T0302010

FOREIGN DIRECT INVESTMENT

INVESTMENT

A Global Perspective

FOREIGN DIRECT INVESTMENT

A Global Perspective

Hwy-Chang Moon

Seoul National University, South Korea

NEW JERSEY · LONDON · SINGAPORE · BEIJING · SHANGHAI · HONG KONG · TAIPEI · CHENNAI · TOKYO

Published by

World Scientific Publishing Co. Pte. Ltd.
5 Toh Tuck Link, Singapore 596224
USA office: 27 Warren Street, Suite 401-402, Hackensack, NJ 07601
UK office: 57 Shelton Street, Covent Garden, London WC2H 9HE

Library of Congress Cataloging-in-Publication Data
Mun, Hwi-ch'ang.
   Foreign direct investment : a global perspective / Hwy-Chang Moon, Seoul National University, South Korea.
     pages cm
   Includes bibliographical references and index.
   ISBN 978-9814583602 (hardcover) -- ISBN 981458360X (hardcover)
   1. Investments, Foreign. 2. International business enterprises. I. Title.
   HG4538.F6183 2015
   332.67'3--dc23

                       2014039437

British Library Cataloguing-in-Publication Data
A catalogue record for this book is available from the British Library.

In-house Editor: Philly Lim

Typeset by Stallion Press
Email: enquiries@stallionpress.com

Printed in Singapore

Preface

The conventional theory of foreign direct investment (FDI) is to view the motivation of FDI as "exploiting" the ownership or monopolistic advantages of multinational corporations (MNCs) in an industry which has a high degree of market failure. In this exploitative world of MNC operations, countries may be adversely affected. However, in today's more complicated and competitive environment of business, MNCs are more willing to co-create values through "sharing and learning" with home and host countries by constructing a global ecosystem, rather than just to exploit their advantages. In this cooperative world, both MNCs and countries will benefit. I have confirmed this new compelling perspective through my related consulting projects and extensive studies on this subject. It is now imperative to broaden our scope of analysis on the operation of MNCs and their impact on countries.

This book is different from existing studies particularly as it relates to some important points. First, most of the existing studies focus on FDI from developed country MNCs, i.e., the Western perspective, but this book deals with both developing and developed country MNCs, i.e., the global perspective. Second, this book focuses more on cooperating than competing nature of multinational activities between firms and countries, thereby enhancing synergies between them and creating new business opportunities. Third, this book extends the conventional perspectives on other important topics, including foreign entry modes, clusters, and creating shared value on both the firm and country level. In addition, this book not only add values to academia, but also gives useful strategic implications for both business managers and policy makers.

For the publication of this book, I would like to give special thanks to Sohyun Yim, who has helped me from the beginning to the end of this project. Without her dedication, this book could not have been completed within a reasonable timeframe. Thanks also go to Jimmyn Parc, Sylvain Rémy, Wenyan Yin, and Yeon Woo Lee, who have contributed to some parts of this book in a close consultation with me. In addition, I would like to thank the editorial staff members of World Scientific Publishing Co., for their valuable help in publishing this book.

Hwy-Chang Moon
Seoul National University

Contents

Introduction

Trade balance no longer represents the economic performance of a nation; rather it is at best a distorted and at worst a wrong picture of national competitiveness. It is because multinational corporations (MNCs) have become increasingly mobile and input resources are mobilized everywhere. Firms build competitive advantages by investing their activities and finding new resources on a global basis, and this can enhance the national competitiveness as well. Such activities of MNCs are called foreign direct investment (FDI).

FDI theories were mainly developed from the traditional economic perspectives on market failures by tackling the underlying assumption of neo-classical trade theories, i.e., the perfect market system and factor immobility across national borders. Hymer, the grandfather of FDI studies, averred that MNCs grow in order to exploit their monopolistic assets in foreign locations, thus need to be regulated further deteriorate structural market failure. On the other hand, Williamson regarded that transaction-cost-based market failure is endemic, so that MNCs need to be encouraged to make market transactions more efficient.

Dunning, who established the backbone of FDI theories, has incorporated both economic perspectives on market failures and business perspectives of value creation. Dunning's theory was initially developed from Hymer's monopolistic assets to explain why firms invest abroad (later named as ownership advantage), then he identified location-specific advantage to explain where MNCs choose to invest. Although Dunning explained that the main purpose of FDI is to exploit ownership advantages in foreign locations, he acknowledged the importance of internalizing the market for MNCs to grow and enhance their current ownership advantages. Thus he added the third ladder and called this the internalization advantage to explain how firms engage in foreign operations. The three advantages together formed the tripods of the ownership-location-internalization (OLI) paradigm and became very useful to explain why MNCs from developed countries invest in developing countries (downward investments).

Despite Dunning's contribution to FDI studies, the OLI paradigm is based on the firms from developed countries that already possess ownership advantages. From the late 20th century, however, firms from developing countries started investing in developed countries (upward investments), without any significant ownership advantages compared to other MNCs from developed countries. In the world of Dunning's conventional OLI paradigm, these upward investments were rather regarded as an exceptional phenomenon.

To explain this unconventional phenomenon, Moon and Roehl introduced the imbalance theory based on Penrose's perception that the imbalances in resource portfolio make firm grow. They applied her perception to international business and claimed that it is not only the advantage of the firm but the imbalances of the firm resources that motivate firms to invest abroad to address the current imbalances. Both affluence and deficiency of resources will motivate firms to go abroad, but the deficiency will stimulate firms more for their survival and for overcoming critical disadvantage of the firm. The imbalance theory does not only overcome limitations of OLI paradigm but also gives a significant implication that firms need to constantly balance out any of the imbalances that reside in their value chain.

The imbalance theory can also further be applied to host country's strategic policies to attract the most competitive MNCs and maximize their spillover effects. The host country needs to provide a business environment in attracting MNCs to utilize their advantages while also complementing their disadvantages. The most effective way of achieving these two goals is to build a cluster to exchange resources and knowledge. The cluster usually is referred to as firm networks that are situated spatially close to each other, but it can be expanded to the networks of clusters across regional and national boundaries. The global linkage between Silicon Valley in the US and Bangalore in India is a good example.

The competitiveness of clusters can be enhanced from the four endogenous determinants of Porter's diamond model (factor conditions, demand conditions, related and supporting industries, and firm strategy, structure & rivalry), and two exogenous determinants (government and chance). These interactive determinants together form a self-reinforcing mechanism of creating sources of locational competitive advantage. Although the diamond model was originally introduced to analyze the competitiveness of national industries, this model can be utilized and extended as a tool for analyzing locational attractiveness for global managers. This book introduces new extended models that were utilized to assess locational attractiveness. The case studies of Korea and Azerbaijan were conducted to give strategic implications for both global managers to choose the most appropriate investment locations and for policy makers to develop attractive business environments.

Not only choosing the appropriate location is important but how to enter the location is critical. Firms can either externalize or internalize foreign markets. Externalization is to engage in arm's length transactions through trade or licensing, while internalization is to engage in a certain level of equity or control over a foreign firm through forming strategic alliances or joint ventures, or setting up a wholly owned subsidiary. Internalization theory or the entry mode choice was initially analyzed from the market failure perspective, yet by adding locational factors and complementarity, we can explain different internalization modes as well as different externalization modes (e.g., inter-firm trade, intra-firm trade, and licensing).

Although scholars and practitioners are finding more positive rationale for the MNC activities, the FDI impacts on both host and home countries have been controversial. There may be more positive impacts of FDI on both the host and home countries that can outweigh possible negative impacts. However, negative impacts cannot be ignored. With growing public awareness as well as institutional pressures on the environmental and social issues, firms need to seek ways not only to mitigate negative impacts but also to find new business opportunities by solving critical disadvantages at the home and host countries. This is the so-called "creating shared values (CSV)" between MNCs and both the home and host countries. Firms finding social opportunities will foster cooperation towards creating new sources of competitiveness together with the home and host countries, so that firms can reduce tensions with the national governments and continue to generate new sources of competitive advantages.

All of the chapters of this book highlight the changing perspectives regarding FDI such as from western multinationals to global firms, from traditional theory to new theory, from local to global link, and from responsibility to opportunity. The readers of this book can thus understand the past, present, and future of the strategic issues regarding FDI and global value chain of business.

Chapter 1

International Players: From Western Multinationals to Global Firms

Summary

There are no firms or industries that are purely domestic. Most of the goods that are accessible in the marketplace are now "made in world." Yet we have a very limited view on how global firms and industries have emerged. For a better understanding of the strategies in the business world, different kinds of international firms are introduced. Their strategies may be regional or global, standardized or diversified (localized) depending on physical and psychic distances. Both physical and psychic distances, however, should not be taken as a cost of foreignness but a source of new opportunities. In this chapter, we will see how international firms have evolved to take advantage of these new opportunities.

1.1. National Interest vs. National Allegiance

Over the several decades, firms have learned that they can benefit largely from foreign production. They can dramatically lower their production costs, increase their foreign demands for their products, and explore new markets (Farrell, 2004). Their influence stretches far beyond national boundaries, and the international competition has changed.

Let's take a look at the case of aircraft production as shown in Figure 1.1.[1] There are only two aircraft producers in the world, the Airbus from the EU

---

[1] Doors and windows, escape slides, engine nacelles, and auxiliary power units are made in the US, whereas flight deck seats (UK), passenger doors (France), and cargo doors

1

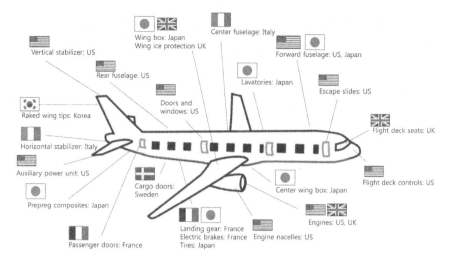

Figure 1.1   Boeing Aircraft: Made in World
Source: Meng and Miroudot (2011).

and Boeing from the US. Although the market looks as if the competition exists between the EU and the US, the actual competition takes place in a global arena. Parts and components of the Boeing aircrafts are produced from around the world. The aircraft buyers (airline and transportation companies) and end customers (travelers) are spread all around the world, so it is almost impossible to determine the nationality of the product or the company. Products and services are "made in world" and serve the worldwide market in which firm competitiveness arises based on how these two firms can manage their made-in-world products.

Then how can we understand the changing nature of business competition? How are businesses taking place in the global economy? Let us assume that there are two firms. Firm A has directors and shareholders from America but operates in a foreign country, South Korea. On the other hand, Firm B has directors and shareholders from Korea and its operations

(Sweden) are made in Europe. For stabilizers, vertical stabilizer is made in the US, horizontal stabilizer is made in Italy. Raked wing tips are made in Korea. Japan also takes a large part in aircraft production. Lavatories, forward fuselage, center wing box, pre-preg composites as well as tires and wing box are made in Japan.

are mostly based in America and its R&D center is situated in Silicon Valley. Now, which of the two companies is American or Korean?

Firm A is owned by Americans (American shareholders) but it has less relevance to American economy and competitiveness. It hires few Americans and creates values outside of America. On the other hand, firm B is owned by Koreans but is contributing more to the American economy and employment. Its operations and sales are created in America. Therefore, despite the nationality of ownership, the company that adds more values to the American economy is firm B.

Some may argue that ownership and control can determine the nationality of the firm. For example, firm A will try to maximize benefits for American investors. Also, American managers, although they may operate in foreign companies, will act in the best interest of America. Yet, would American managers put national interest before the firm's interest? The marketplace does not spare room for national allegiance when it comes to a matter of survival in global competition. The reality is that global managers make decisions of the location that will provide the most benefits to the company, even if the decision benefits the foreign country more than it does for America (Reich, 1990).

Firms behave on behalf of their own interests, not by national allegiance, unless the company is closely tied to their nation's economic development, either through direct public ownership or through financial intermediaries (Reich, 1990). They may want to contribute to national development but there may incur large inefficiencies. Furthermore, the government would not be capable of such detailed oversight of the firms. In the end, firms have to seek competitive strategies to pursue a lower cost or a higher value creation to sustain their competitiveness, which means to look for business opportunities both inside and outside the national boundaries that serve their interests better.

What about the host countries? The government policies, when devising strategies to benefit the national interest, must gear towards fostering a favorable business environment that can attract global firms to bring in foreign capital, technology, entrepreneurship as well as the technical know-how (Reich, 1991). The nationality of the firm which brings in these valuable resources to the country does not matter as long as it contributes to the national economy. Thus, developing national competitiveness lies in developing national policies that reward global corporation and foster a business-friendly environment for global companies, regardless of their nationality.

Some may argue that the market equates the value and attitude towards the product with the economic level or perceived value of the country-of-origin. Yet, as the market becomes more competitive, national allegiance decreases in the market place. The market has become much more informed about the product and consumers choose and buy based on their opportunistic behavior. They try to maximize their own values rather than stick to the national allegiance. Thus, firm operations are not limited to the national or regional boundaries and they need to seek resources and capabilities that can best serve the market by providing cost-effective or differentiated values in the global arena.

1.2. Global Diversification of FDI

In the past, firms were engaged in foreign production, but their foreign operations remained as subsidiaries to the headquarters that were based in the country of the parent company (Reich, 1990). In recent times, cross-border ownership has boomed, and their headquarters are not necessarily based in their country of origin. There are multiple businesses which are spread across international strategic regions. The high value-added activities, including R&D centers, are also situated where the knowledge is highly concentrated and their production sites are relocated in places that are most cost-effective and strategically important.

The MNCs we see nowadays have their origins from the firms born out of the second industrial revolution in the late 19th century (Guillen and Garcia-Canal, 2009). In earlier years, firms were taking global strategies to exploit natural resources for export or to supply foreign markets with similar products to those produced at home (Dunning, 2001b). The amount of investment was limited and the targeted industries or regions were peripheral.

The expansion of Western firms started from the end of the 1950s when trade and investment barriers gradually fell around the world (Chandler, 1990). The multinationals from the US and the European countries started to increase, mainly to serve the Western markets. Their investments started to diversify into the less developed countries, seeking cost reductions, mainly in ex-colony countries, however, they remained unilateral. No investment flows were seen from these countries into the US and the EU. This is why FDI studies were mainly conducted on the Western firms and focused on unilateral exploitation of firm resources and advantages.

The first non-Western players were the Japanese firms that posed new threats to the Western firms. The Japanese firms did not only invest in the Western market for knowledge sourcing and market access, but also in Southeast Asian markets for a lower production cost. Their investment increased with their successful penetration into the Western markets but was also stimulated by trade barriers set upon Japanese products. Because the inflow of Japanese products was increasing in the Western market, the host governments imposed various trade barriers; mainly the anti-dumping duties that made the Japanese firms use circumventing strategies to maintain their sales in the Western market.

After the 1990s, FDI volume started increasing from the newly industrializing economies such as Spain, Portugal, South Korea, and Taiwan as well as from oil rich countries such as United Arab Emirates, Nigeria, and Venezuela. In later stages, emerging large countries such as China, Brazil, Mexico, India, and Turkey, and Southeast Asian countries such as Indonesia and Thailand also started large amounts of outward FDI (Guillen and Garcia-Canal, 2009). Thus, the global investment is not limited from the traditional triad regions: the US, the EU and Japan but takes place around the world. Firm productions are distributed across national borders and form a complex web of FDI. The targeted location of FDI has also diversified as the internationalization is becoming real.

1.3. Globalization vs. Regionalization

In terms of economic and cultural dependence, globalization is an inevitable phenomenon. Yet, the degree of globalization is a different story. Indeed, some scholars such as Rugman and Verbeke (2004; 2008) argued that globalization is skewed.[2] Global business activities are dispersed and

---

[2] Rugman and Verbeke (2008) also tested the multinational firms in service industries and showed similar results to the earlier research conducted in 2004.

operated in the areas that are regionally or culturally close. Their study is not much different from what Kenichi Ohmae insisted in his book called *Triad Powers* in 1985, explaining the "global impasse" of the triad regions. The triads are: the US, the EU, and Japan, where Ohmae observed that these three regions are the main pillars of the global economy.

Rugman and Verbeke (2004) examined the world's largest MNCs (Fortune 500) and where their sales are largely created. They showed that during the 1980s, firms created sales in one or two of the three regions of the EU, the US, and Japan. Among the Fortune 500, 135 firms operated in their home region, with no sales elsewhere. Twenty five firms had sales in two of the three regions and only nine were global, in all three regions, including Coca-Cola (ranked as 129th) and McDonald's (ranked as 350th). The rest of the firms were ambiguous due to lack of data.

Such uneven distribution of MNCs' sales across the globe shows that there are limitations in transferring firm-specific resources while being advantageous for some regions. Firms lack the capability to internalize the foreign market and deal with local policies because they become less competent in markets where the structures and policies are unfamiliar.

After Rugman and Verbeke published their paper in 2004, Dunning, Fujita, and Yakova (2007), while appreciating the micro-analysis, examined the macro perspective on regionalization and globalization. Dunning, Fujita, and Yakova (2007) improved and adopted new research methods; using three indexes, namely, transnationality index (TI), globalization index (GI) and the revealed investment comparative advantage (RICA).[3] The classification of the regions used by Dunning, Fujita, and Yakova (2007) was also revised from the Triad to six clusters of countries based on geographical distances, country size (GDP), and psychic distances as well

---

[3] The first index is the TI which is used to assess the degree of a country's outward or inward FDI. The TI uses the percentage of foreign assets, sales, and employment accounted by the foreign affiliates. The second index is the GI, which attempts to assess the extent to which the geographical spread of inward and outward FDI is concentrated or dispersed. The third index is the RICA or investment intensity index. This is to measure the extent to which, relative to its share of the world direct investment stock, a country's outward investment in a number of culturally different geographical regions is above or below the average.

as institutional differences.[4] The categories are: Anglo cluster, Germanic/ Nordic cluster, Latin American cluster, Latin European cluster, Far Eastern cluster, and "Other or Mixed" cluster, which includes all other countries.[5]

Yet, despite the differences and improved methodologies, the results were similar in that firm investments were not well diversified. Geographically speaking, some regions have comparative/absolute advantages in certain aspects, such as knowledge intensity, technology concentration, and so on, whereas many firms also agglomerate in certain regions to protect or enhance their technological, organizational, and managerial competencies.

Despite similar results regarding firms' tendency on regionalization, there are major differences between Rugman and Vebeke (2004; 2008) and Dunning, Fujita, and Yakova (2007) works. Rugman and Verbeke (2004; 2008) looked into "the locus of destination" that is the geographic distribution of downstream activities, where Dunning, Fujita and Yakova (2007) included both the downstream and upstream activities of the firm. Then how can we systematically understand global investment pattern? What do we mean by a global firm or global strategy? In order to address these questions, it is important to understand the basics of firm operations and different types of global firms.

1.4. Different Types of Global Strategy and Global Firms

Firms have been engaged in international activities in one way or another. Whether they are geographically concentrated or dispersed is a matter of how firms design their international production and target markets.

---

[4] This was used by other scholars such as Ronen and Shenkar (1985).

[5] The six regional clusters are as follows. (1) Anglo: Australia, Canada, Ireland, New Zealand, South Africa, US, UK (2) Latin European: Belgium, France, Italy, Portugal, Spain (3) Nordic and Germanic: Austria, Denmark, Finland, Germany, Netherlands, Norway, Sweden, Switzerland (4) Latin American: Argentina, Brazil, Chile, Colombia, Mexico, Peru, Venezuela (5) Far Eastern: China, Hong Kong, India, Indonesia, Japan, Korea, Malaysia, Philippines, Singapore, Taiwan, Thailand and (6) Other (all the rest).

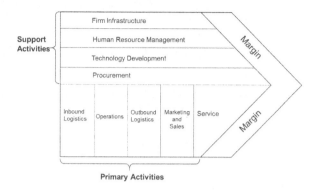

Figure 1.2   Porter's (1985) Value Chain

To analyze why firms show different paths of internationalization, let's look into the generic value chain of firms (see Figure 1.2).

Porter's (1985) generic value chain portrays the streams of many discrete activities of firm operation. Firms design, produce, and provide various services such as marketing, delivery, and after sales support. Each activity is called as the value activity, which can be categorized into primary and support activities. Primary activities are those involved in the physical creation of the product, its sales, and its transfer to the buyer as well as after-sales support. Support activities are the ones that assist the primary activities by providing procurement, technology, human resources, and firm infrastructure.

Among the primary activities of the firm, inbound logistics, operations, and outbound logistics are associated with "inputs" management and they are referred to as the "upstream activities" of the firm. Marketing and sales as well as service, which deal more directly with end buyers, are referred to as the "downstream activities" of a firm. Porter (1985) said that the competitive advantage of a firm derives from how a firm can manage its value chain activities in a better way.

The activities may vary among firms. Firms specialize in one of the activities of the value chain, thus each of the value activities can be sub-categorized. For example, a firm's marketing and sales activity can be divided into marketing management, advertising, sales force administration and operations, and promotion (see Figure 1.3).

These specialized firms also outsource certain value activities or cooperate with other firms to form an industry value chain (see Figure 1.4).

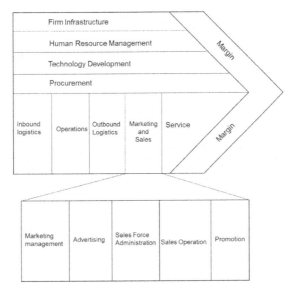

Figure 1.3 Sub-categorization of Each Value Activity
Sources: Porter (1985), and Moon (2010).

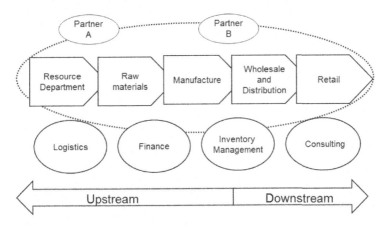

Figure 1.4 Industry Value Chain
Source: Moon (2010).

For example, suppliers, final goods providers, and marketing and sales firms are all independent but work together to complete an industry value chain. Firms in charge of resource development, raw materials, and manufacturing are the upstream firms of the industry value chain, whereas firms that manage wholesale, distribution, and retail are the downstream firms.

Cooperation among firms goes beyond the national boundaries. Regardless of firm nationality, firms seek competitive partners to make their industry value chain competitive. This is why there cannot be any industry that is purely domestic and any part of the value chain activities can be performed in foreign locations.

Then, which firms are global firms? We use various terminologies for international firms such as multi-domestic, multinational, global, or trans-national firms. At one extreme, there is a multi-domestic firm that tailors firm strategies and products to each local need. Each foreign subsidiary shows distinctive features of the locations and markets. On the other extreme, there is a global firm that implements parent firm strategies and utilizes knowledge retained at the headquarters to provide similar goods globally. With standardized firm strategies and products, firms exploit economies of scale. A transnational firm does both of what multi-domestic and global firms do. The transnational firm has differentiated contribution by national units to integrate worldwide operations. The shared knowledge is developed jointly among its foreign subunits. MNCs are used in various ways yet more specifically they are the half-way type of transnational firms. They are also referred to as multi-focal firms that exploit local opportuni-ties, while retaining some of the common capabilities such as technology and skills. In reality, however, it is very ambiguous to categorize firms into different types because their international activities have evolved and per-formed in diverse ways. Thus, the terminologies to indicate international firms have been used inter-changeably.

Scholars have tried to explain international firm activities from vari-ous perspectives. One aspect to distinguish international firms is to see how firms are integrated and coordinated across different regions and how responsive they are to regional differences. Prahalad and Doz (1987) explai-ned that while firms need to take advantage of global efficiency and exploit market imperfections that are derived from multi-country differences; they need to be responsive to the demands imposed by the competitive government or market forces in each location. Thus, the framework is based on two imperatives: Pressures for global integration and pressures for local responsiveness. This was modeled and named as the integration-respon-siveness (I-R) framework.

Global integration refers to the force that pressures firms to make stra-tegic choices as a collective organization so that the activities are integrated across national boundaries. *Local responsiveness* is the force that necessitates firms to be sensitive to local pressures and respond predominantly to each local market and industry settings. These two pressures force firms to make strategic choices depending on their activities and industry characteristics. Thus, if we were to situate different types of international firms in the I-R model, they would look as shown in Figure 1.5.

Global firms are situated in the upper left where integration of the activities is high and responsiveness is low. In the lower right side of the matrix, there are multi-domestic firms where responsiveness is high and integration of activities is low. These are the two extremes of international strategies. Transnational firms are situated in the upper right quadrant which takes specialized and interdependent activities within the range of integrated and standardized sets of strategies. This is to achieve global efficiency and exploit the firm-specific advantages on a worldwide basis while responding to national differences (Bartlett and Ghoshal, 1999). Yet, firms make selective decisions to integrate or communicate their activities differently and this is why the multinational firm is situated in the middle (See Figure 1.5).

Despite the usefulness of the I-R framework, there are limitations. Because coordination is correlated to the integration of firms, Prahalad and Doz (1987) did not distinguish coordination from integration. However,

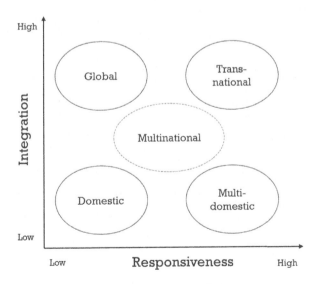

Figure 1.5   I-R Framework and Types of International Firms
Note: This figure was adopted and modified from Prahalad and Doz (1987), and Moon (2010).

even though firms operate in the same market pursuing similar strategies, they may have different property control (coordination) over their firm-specific assets in different regions (Devinney, Midgley, and Venaik, 2000). Moreover, the targeted markets may be similar in characteristics, but they may be geographically distant in reality. This means that the degree of dispersion of firm activities or the number of countries needs to be included in the framework.

In this regard, Porter (1986) introduced a model analyzing the coordination and the linkage across business units and countries. His analysis comes down to configuration and coordination of activities, which is called "the configuration-coordination (C-C) model" (see Figure 1.6). *Configuration* refers to the number of locations in which value chain activities are operated and managed. They can be geographically dispersed or concentrated. *Coordination* is how similar activities of the value chain across national borders are controlled and synergized by the firm.

However, Porter's (1986) C-C Model is not free from criticisms. Country-centered strategy is a totally localized strategy while, export-based strategy is pursued when products are made in one country and exported to foreign markets with low coordination. However, these strategies do not show whether the number of foreign markets are many or a few.

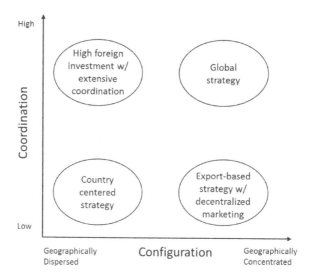

Figure 1.6   Porter's (1986) C-C Model

Global strategy is pursued when products are made in one country and sold in foreign countries with high level of coordination and standardization. Foreign investment strategy shows that the production may be geographically dispersed but it is highly coordinated.

The main problem of this model is not distinguishing between the upstream (production) and downstream (marketing) activities. Thus, Moon (2010) provided an extended model (see Figure 1.7). This model comprises the number of countries to figure out and to what extent the activities are concentrated or dispersed, and the level of coordination of the activities by dividing the upstream and downstream activities of the firm. He explained that, by and large, production-seeking coordination and marketing-seeking coordination are the two ends that firms seek for international strategies.

For example, Toyota is more globalized in marketing, while GM is more globalized in production. These two firms are both regarded to be global firms but are globalized in different aspects. Thus, a distinction between production and marketing shows a more concrete picture of the firms' different global strategies.

Geographical dispersion is not always positive and it is accompanied by costs and risks. At the initial stage of globalization, firms invest in locations that are geographically closer. This is because geographically contiguous

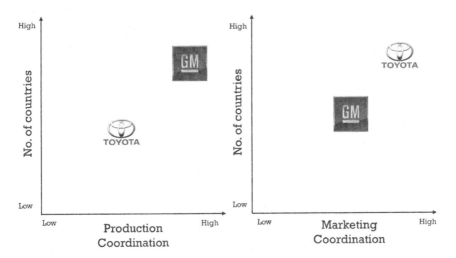

Figure 1.7 Production-seeking and Marketing-seeking Model
Sources: Moon (1994; 2010).

countries are simply perceived to have similar cultures, political and economic systems, and economic development levels (Sethi et al., 2003), which
are foundations for overcoming a psychic distance. Yet, it is a very simplistic
approach because geographical distances do not always equate with psychic
distances. Then, let us take a look at a new map of cultural differences.

1.5. Psychic Distances and New Geography

Psychic distance or unfamiliarity coming from different cultures, laws,
norms, values, political systems, business practices, and economic levels,
shapes global business strategies and determines firms' location choices.
Psychic distance becomes the key barrier to firms' globalization and it
affects direction, performance, and entry mode of the international firms
(Brewer, 2007), because it is perceived as costs associated with foreignness.
Psychic distance can be viewed from two perspectives: Macro and micro.
In the macro perspective, psychic distance comes from history, politics,
economy, as well as educational and religious factors. In the micro perspective, the way of doing business or the organizational structure is the
foundation for dealing with psychic distance. It is difficult to draw a clear
line between the macro and micro perspectives, as they are intertwined
with each other and can affect firm performances in various ways.

This can be seen from the Japanese firms' experience in China. Japanese
were among the first to open factories in China, but they have found difficulty in their business operations due to increasing costs (labor and
administrative costs to deal with labor disputes and stoppage at suppliers)
from incompatibility between Japanese and Chinese despite their geographical proximity. Whereas in the macro aspect, anti-Japanese rioting over
historical grievances has caused great trouble for Japanese businesses, the
micro aspect played critical difficulties in operations in China. For example, Japanese way of management such as Just-In-Time (JIT) production
that made the Japanese firms amazingly efficient elsewhere left them
vulnerable to disruptions in China.

Particularly, the modern Chinese workers, who presume a manager is
empowered to make decisions quickly, have not come to comply with
Japanese managers who have little autonomy and wait for orders from Tokyo
as they operate on consensus-based decision making. Japanese managers,

who have dealt only with loyal, docile, and sacrificing employees at home, have also struggled in training Chinese workers despite their geographical proximity (Economist, 2010). They share different norms and values, religions as well as development paths that make them culturally more distant in doing business than countries that may be physically more apart.

Psychic distances, despite their important roles in international business, were assessed from the Western perspective. In the beginning, psychic distances came from geographical distances. The farther the countries are from the Western countries, the less developed and different the countries become. Distant countries were perceived to be ethnically different, which causes trouble and increased costs for the Western investors (Benito and Gripsrud, 1992). This is why sometimes cultural differences were translated from a chauvinist perspective. This aspect is mentioned in Perlmutter (1969) on cultural differences in international business operations.

1.5.1. *Perlmutter's Cultural Aspects*

An early systematic work on firm motivation for internationalization, based on cultural factors, was done by Perlmutter (1969). He explained that firm strategy can be described in three ways: Ethnocentric (home-country oriented), polycentric (host-country oriented), and geocentric (world-oriented) (see Table 1.1).

Ethnocentric managers (ethnocentricism) believe that the home country's way of doing business is superior and thus should be applied to foreign operations. The perception of doing business in foreign countries is based on "This works at home, therefore it must work in your country" (Perlmutter, 1969). A unilateral counsel or directive flows from headquarters to the subsidiary in a steady stream, and the main functions and workforce are concentrated in headquarters, whereas foreigners are like the "second-class citizens."

Polycentricism on the other hand assumes a foreign country is different and therefore is difficult to understand from the headquarters' perspective. Local managers know the best local way of doing business, thus they should have autonomy from the headquarters. Executives from the headquarters are apt to say "Let Romans do it their way [...] as long as they earn profit, we remain as the background" (Perlmutter, 1969). Polycentricism is about

Table 1.1.   Three Types of Cultural Perspectives between the Headquarters and Subsidiaries

Organization Design	Ethnocentric	Polycentric	Geocentric
Complexity of organization	Complex in home country, simple in subsidiaries	Varied and independent	Increasingly complex and interdependent
Authority and decision making	High in headquarters	Relatively low in headquarters	Aim for a collaborative approach between headquarters and subsidiaries
Evaluation and control	Home standards applied for persons and performances	Determined locally	Find standards which are universal and local
Rewards and punishments	High in headquarters, low in subsidiaries	Wide variation: They can be high or low rewards for subsidiaries	International and local executives rewarded for reaching local and worldwide objectives
Communication (information flow)	High volume to subsidiaries (orders, commands, advice)	Little to and from headquarters. Little between subsidiaries	Both ways and between subsidiaries. Heads of subsidiaries part of management team
Identification	Nationality of owner	Nationality of host country	Truly international company but identifying with national interest
Perpetuation (Recruiting, staffing, development)	Recruit and develop people of home country for key positions everywhere in the world	Develop people of local nationality for key positions in their own country	Develop best men everywhere in the world for key positions everywhere in the world

Source: Perlmutter (1969).

accepting differences but at the same time acknowledging a big barrier in communication and transferring information between the two different cultures of the headquarters and the host country.

Ethnocentric and polycentric executives see that cultural differences prevail from cultural superiority or inferiority, so it is important to build the third aspect — geocentrism. Regardless of nationality, the concept of geocentrism involves a collaborative effort between foreign subsidiaries and home headquarters to establish universal standards and permissible local variables for key strategic decisions (Perlmutter, 1969). Geocentrism is not about superiority of the cultures, but about minimizing cultural costs and creating the maximum value by compromising the best practices of the host and home country cultures (Perlmutter, 1969). This is reflected in the Unilever's board chairman's statement of objectives in India, "We want to Unileverize our Indians and Indianize our Univerans."

In comparing the types of international firms, ethnocentrism is similar to "global strategy" of the firm which coordinates and standardizes the strategies of the headquarters to its foreign subsidiaries; polycentrism is similar to "multi-domestic strategy" which localizes products and business processes to each region; and geocentrism is similar to "transnational strategy" which is perceived to be "idealistic" and inherently unattainable.

Although the role of culture in firm investments and operations is important and unquestionable, isolating it as an independent variable is challenging (Porter, 2000a). It is complex, intangible, and subtle, so it is difficult to scale (Boyacigiller et al., 1996). It is also important to note that cultural distances do not come from the differences in ethnicity or geographical distances. Cultures can be different within a region or similar across different regions. Hofstede (1980; 1983) was one of the most renowned scholars to distinguish economic and cultural factors that explain psychic distances.

1.5.2. *Hofstede's Cultural Dimensions*[6]

Hofstede (1980; 1983) tried to find typical patterns of cultural differences and he first came down to four different dimensions: (1) individualism or

---

[6]Information on Hofstede's models is well documented in http://geerthofstede.com/dimensions.html. This part is largely based on the national realm of culture, yet, Hofstede has also pointed out eight dimensions for organizational culture. They are (1) means oriented or goal oriented, (2) internally driven or externally driven, (3) easygoing work discipline or strict work discipline, (4) local or professional, (5) open or closed systems, (6) employee oriented or work oriented, (7) degree of acceptance of leadership style, and (8) degree of identification with your organization.

collectivism, (2) large or small power distance, (3) strong or weak uncertainty avoidance, and (4) masculinity or femininity. Individualism refers to the social frameworks that take care of oneself and immediate family members, while collectivism represents a society that looks after the members in a group in a tightly-knit social framework. A small power distance means relatively equalized distribution of power among members in the society and a high power distance accepts hierarchy or unequal distribution of power among members. A society with high uncertainty avoidance does not accept any unorthodox behaviors or ideas that can bring any risks in the future, whereas low uncertainty avoidance represents the opposite. Masculinity represents a society that honors heroism, assertiveness, and material rewards for success and competition. Feminism stands for modesty and care for the weak as well as for quality of life and cooperation among society members.

After a decade, Hofstede became fascinated by Confucianism in China and added a fifth dimension which is short-term/long-term orientation in his book (Hofstede, 1991). The fifth dimension was incorporated and revised in the study conducted by Hofstede and his coworkers in 2010, and was changed to the pragmatic or normative tendencies of people. The short-term orientated people seek the absolute truth and focus on achieving quick results. Thus, they are more normative. The long-term orientated people seek virtuous life rather than searching for the truth. They believe that much of the truth depends on the situation, context, and time. They accept contradictions and show a strong propensity to save and invest for the future, as well as perseverance for getting results (Hofstede, Hofstede, and Minkov, 2010).

When the fifth dimension was revised, Hofstede and his coworkers also added the sixth dimension that is indulgence versus restraint (Hofstede, Hofstede, and Minkov, 2010). The indulgence refers to the human drives related to enjoying life and having fun and the restraint refers to the society that suppresses gratification of needs by means of strict social norms.

1.5.3. *Moon's OUI Model*

Hofstede's six dimensions of cultural factors are independent variables and they are all measured in relative scales. He also introduced organizational cultural factors apart from six national cultural dimensions. Despite his great contribution, his cultural factors are criticized for being not mutually exclusive with each other. To solve this problem and add missing variables, Moon (2004a) introduced the Openness, Uncertainty Avoidance, Individualism (OUI) model (see Table 1.2).

Among Hofstede's cultural dimensions, Moon (2004a) explained that there exist high correlations between the three; countries with large "power distance" tend to have low "individualism" and high "long-term orientation." For example, individualistic society is responsible for one's conduct which gives rewards based on individual merit system rather than hierarchical position (low power distance) and on tangible short-term performance. Collectivist society, on the other hand, is based more on the social or inherited hierarchical status to maintain hierarchical

Table 1.2. The OUI Model and Its Cultural Variables

Cultural Variables	Sub-variables	Proxy Variables
Openness	Aggressiveness	International changes
		Global standards
		Willingness to accept new ideas
	Attractiveness	Equal treatment
		Professional job's openness
		MNC's activities (inward FDI)
Uncertainty Avoidance	Disciplinism	Public order
		Bureaucracy
		Bribery and corruption
	Frontierism	Innovation and creativity
		Entrepreneur's core competencies
		Ability to seize opportunities
Individualism	Responsibility	Job description and individual role
		Corporate governance
		The relationship between labor and management
	Reward	Reward system
		Firms' decision process
		Professional compensation

Source: Moon (2004a).

order (high power distance) which emphasizes long-term stability rather than short-term achievement.

Descriptions under the "masculinity/femininity" dimension are also highly overlapping with the ones under "individualism/collectivism." For example, masculinity that comprises aspects of competition and femininity of cooperation tend to overlap with a tendency to seek individual or collective gains. Thus, Moon (2004a) reorganized three dimensions of Hofstede's model (low power distance, individualism, and masculinity versus high power distance, collectivism, and femininity) into one variable of "Individualism" and sub-categorized it to "Reward" and "Responsibility."

On the other hand, Hofstede's "Uncertainty Avoidance" variable was extended to include "Disciplinism" and "Frontierism." Disciplinism is a tendency to maintain order and, therefore, tends to have a low degree of corruption and a high degree of restraint (i.e., low degree of indulgence). Frontierism, on the other hand, is concerned with challenging and exploring undeveloped fields which have close relationships with innovativeness and creativity. Although Moon's OUI model was introduced prior to the introduction of Hofstede's sixth dimension, Moon's extended "Uncertainty Avoidance" factor covers the aspect of the sixth dimension as well. Restriction goes under Disciplinism, and Indulgence goes under Frontierism.

Moon (2004a), with an understanding on cultures of small countries or fast growing Asian countries, introduced a new variable, "Openness." These countries with lack of natural resources could achieve their economic development through creating new competitive advantages, because they were very open to internationalization. Singapore and South Korea are good examples (see Chapter 2). The Openness variable is subdivided into Aggressiveness and Attractiveness. A quick adaptation to international changes and global standards as well as accepting new ideas is "aggressive" way of being open, and accepting professional jobs and investments as well as giving equal treatments towards foreigners and foreignness is regarded as an "attractive" way of being open.

As cultural factors or psychic distances are important for international business, scholars have applied these factors to innovation, in organizational transaction, technology transfer, the sequence of foreign investments, and entry modes (Shenkar, 2001). Yet, the correlation with cultural factors shows different results among studies: Positive, negative or no relations.

This can be explained by a lack of consensus in defining cultural and psychic distances as well as methodologies and data sets (Shenkar, 2001).

Moon (2004a), on the other hand, said that OUI factors are closely related to the competitiveness of nations, measured by the composite index of the IPS model (see Chapter 7). The higher openness, uncertainty avoidance, and individualism a nation has, the more competitive the nation becomes. Thus, when managing cultural factors, it is not only crucial to improve OUI factors within the national boundary, but also to make them competitive for doing business across countries.

Countries with different degrees in OUI variables will cause conflicts despite their geographical proximity. Yet, finding complementary cultural aspects among countries can pave a way for further growth. For example, the East Asian bloc shows different strengths in different pillars of the OUI model (see Figure 1.8). Japanese show strengths in Individualism, Chinese in Openness, and Koreans in Uncertainty Avoidance (Moon, 2004a). Although

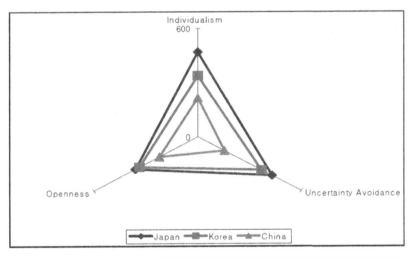

	Japan	Korea	China
Individualism	468.99	338.38	214.08
Uncertainty Avoidance	429.77	369.58	152.60
Openness	356.27	337.95	222.57

Figure 1.8 Cultural Competitiveness and Distances between Japan, Korea, and China
Source: Moon (2004a).

Japanese have the highest indexes in all three OUI pillars compared to those of Korea and China, the comparative strengths in these countries show a potential for frictions. Yet, when managed well, these cultural differences can give new insights and business opportunities for cooperation. Cultural diversity thus has become one of the factors contributing to organizational creativity and innovation as well as a source of competitive advantage rather than causing friction.[7]

Psychic distances along with the geographical distances have initially been analyzed in terms of the cost analysis. The farther the countries are geographically, the more the countries become distant in terms of cultures, incurring high administration and hidden costs. Just as physical distances have been reduced by the development of transportation and communication technologies, psychic distances can also be overcome. In the end, reducing psychic distances is not only a matter of cost reduction, but also a matter of learning and creating new business opportunities. Increased level of knowledge on a foreign country reduces both the cost and uncertainty in foreign markets (Buckley and Casson, 1981; Benito and Gripsrud, 1992). At the same time, more knowledge on host countries accumulates to the diversity of knowledge stock that becomes a source of competitive advantage (see Chapter 2).

1.6. Conclusion

Globalization has become an inevitable trend, but few existing studies have shown a good understanding of globalization. This chapter illustrates what globalization is and how it has changed the business landscape of firm competition. Firms do not just compete competing domestically; they source foreign production inputs and sell their products in foreign markets to survive and prosper in global competition. Firms pursue different international strategies that may change over time.

Although physical and psychic distances were conventionally considered as costs and barriers in business operations, with technological

---

[7] Advocates on "value in cultural diversity" insist that exposure to different cultures stimulates new perspectives and creativity. Understanding various cultures also helps firms be flexible in different business operations and enhance problem solving skills (Cox and Blake, 1991).

advancement and an increased level of knowledge of foreign locations, they have become the source of accumulating diverse knowledge stocks and new business opportunities. Firms can gain new knowledge stock which will help firms upgrade and innovate while they can also expand the overseas markets to increase their performance.

According to the conventional Western FDI theories, firms go abroad to exploit their own firm-specific advantages (see Chapter 3). In the increasingly globalized business environment of today, not just Western firms, but also developing country firms actively go abroad. However, their motivations are often quite different from the conventional Western perspective. These new global firms go abroad to get access to strategic assets such as technology and brand name rather than just to exploit their existing advantages (see Chapter 4). It is time to expand the scope of analysis from a Western to a global perspective.

Chapter 2

International Business Strategy: From Trade to FDI

Summary

We have looked at the changing nature of firms and business landscapes due to physical and psychic distances. Whereas physical and psychic distances were a matter of operational costs of doing business abroad, they have evolved to become the source of new business opportunities. As an extension of "cost reduction" perspective to "learning" perspective, we delve into theoretical foundations for international transactions, starting from the distinction between the conventional means of trade and the new means of Foreign Direct Investment (FDI). This chapter introduces then how we can understand the competitiveness of a nation and a firm by incorporating the concept of internationalization. The evolution of theoretical foundation from economic to business perspectives gives a more rigorous and comprehensive understanding of FDI and firm operations in changing business environment.

2.1. Two Means of International Transactions

2.1.1. Trade[1]

In the past, firms were mainly engaged in international transactions through arm's length exporting and importing. This means that products were produced domestically and sold outside the national boundary. In later stages, firms started engaging in international production. What was the reason for firms to move outside of the national boundary?

---

[1] This part was abstracted and extended from Cho and Moon (2013a).

Trade theories were developed based on the perfect market system. The mercantilist economic perspective of zero-sum game, where one's gain comes from the other's loss, does not take into account of the value creation of firms. This perspective assumes that in order for a country to prosper, it needs to export more than import, which encourages domestic production. This is how trade balance has become the representative measure of national wealth that needs to be regulated and advocated under the economic nationalism.

After mercantilist's view on world trade was Adam Smith's absolute advantage model based on natural law and invisible hand. Smith saw international trade is indeed not a zero-sum but a positive-sum game. The market participants, as long as they specialize in what they are good at, can maximize the overall pie of the wealth of trading partners. However, according to this theory, only the strong ones, which have absolute advantages, can survive and the weak ones cannot gain from international trade. Despite the great contribution by Smith to increasing efficiency through specialization, absolute advantage theory could not fully provide a persuasive explanation of why countries are still engaged in international trade as many countries do not have any absolute advantages.

This was later solved by David Ricardo who posited that nations without an absolute advantage can also benefit through trade when they specialize in the sectors which have "comparative" advantages, or less disadvantages. This is because nations have to think about the opportunity cost when calculating the growth of national wealth. It is not only about how much one produces but also about how much it does not lose. The country will specialize in the industry with less inferiority, so it can minimize the disadvantage and complement it through international trade. The relative sense of advantages was calculated in terms of labor productivity. Then why does the labor productivity differ across industries and nations? Why do some countries have different disadvantages or advantages in resources?

To explain the differences in comparative advantage of nations, Eli Heckscher and Bertil Ohlin at the Stockholm School of Economics built on the Ricardian model and explained that it is because the factor endowments vary across nations. Factor endowment perspective regards that nations differ based on the factor inputs a nation possesses and goods differ based on which factors are used for production of those goods. Thus, the intensity of the resources endowed in the production will be determined by the comparative advantage of factor endowments a nation has. Heckscher–Ohlin model became the basis of factor price equalization that was initially presented by Wolfgang Stolper and Paul Samuelson. The factor price equalization theory posits that the price of factor inputs will be equalized in the end through free international trade.

All these trade theories have been very influential and useful, yet the assumption is that countries have to stick to their current state of advantages they have at home. There are two reasons for this. First, trade theories assume that factor mobility is possible only within the national boundary but not across the boundary. This is why Ricardian model is about comparative advantage between the two industries within a nation, rather than between nations. Second, because countries specialize in what they are (comparatively) good at, they continue focusing on what they do, which gives them no incentive for additional industry upgrade or change. Thus, trade theories cannot explain why some countries show structural changes in export industries and why some countries outperform others over time.

Let us take an example of Korea's economic development. Korea has achieved 300 times of economic growth (GDP per capita) from 1960 (less than 100 US dollars of per capita GDP) to 2014 (approximately 30,000 US dollars), within half a century. Its economic growth can be explained by trade theories: high productivity and high export volumes. What cannot be explained yet is Korea's upgrade of industrial structures that took place in almost every decade.

After the Korean War ended in 1953, the Korean economy was devastated. The country had only primary industries such as agriculture which were not enough in quantity to support the whole nation, nor good in quality to serve (foreign) markets. Yet, under the president Park Chung-Hee's economic planning, Korea started developing light industries and exported wigs and textiles. From the 1970s, Korean firms started exporting radios and black and white TV sets that were produced domestically as original equipment manufacturer (OEM) of US and Japanese MNCs. The export boom gradually paved a way to heavy industries where the government found the importance of basic materials such as iron and steel as the backbone of a modern industrial economy.

By 1981, Korea's domestic steel capacity covered 90% of the domestic markets and some steel products were already being exported (Moon, 2012b). To vertically deepen the industrial structure, the machinery and equipment industry development was accelerated. This consequently gave a boost to the growth of electronics industry, starting from assembly line of parts and components to production of complete consumer goods (Moon, 2012b). Benefited largely from heavy and chemical industries, Korean conglomerates were able to adopt technologies from abroad and make a qualitative leap to the high value-added industries of semiconductor. In the 2000s, Korea was leading in most of its strategic industries, from steel, electronics, and semiconductor to shipbuilding.

Korea's economic growth comes from investing in generative sectors that link industries and sources of technological and organizational innovations that spread to other sectors (Bunker and Ciccantell, 2007). This shows factor mobility across industries. Moreover, Korea adopted talents from abroad and brought in foreign technologies. Particularly, inter-country mobility of experts played a significant role in transferring tacit knowledge (World Bank, 1993; Chesbrough, 1999).

Then how would trade theories explain such phenomenon of industry change? One aspect that trade theories can explain is that the Korean economy grew from trade surplus. Yet large exports were rather a result of industry structural change rather than the driver for the change. The industry structure change cannot be explained by trade theories as they do not incorporate foreign investment or active factor mobility across national borders. Rather the change can be better explained by FDI theories.

2.1.2. *FDI*

FDI, simply put, is an investment activity of a firm taken outside of the country-of-origin. This is different from trade because trade is an exchange of final or intermediary goods which does not entail any kinds of management or control over foreign production. FDI is an exchange of factor inputs and its transaction involves a certain level of management (equity investments).[2]

---

[2]This is different from investments made only in capital, like portfolio investments. They are called as indirect investment as opposed to direct investment. (Moon, 2004a).

The basic assumptions of trade theories were perfect market system, price equalization in factor and goods market, and immobile factor inputs across countries. They assume that there are no transportation costs, no information costs, and no barriers to competition. The markets have identical tastes, and there are constant returns to scale (Rugman, 1980; Cho and Moon, 2013a; Calvet, 1981). Because of these characteristics, there is no incentive for resource mobility across nations. The resources are available to everyone and completely mobile within the nation, so foreign production cannot be included in the picture of trade theories.

FDI theories assume the opposite. The world market is imperfect, no factor price equalization or goods price equalization has been observed and factor inputs are mobile across nations, driven by MNCs. Because the prices of factors and goods are not equalized across nations, firms go abroad to fully take advantage of their competitive assets in foreign countries. They transfer technology, capital, and entrepreneurship across national borders so as to exploit their advantages as they do in their home countries. Their benefits increase if firms can exploit their non-disposable firm-specific in foreign countries. For example, entrepreneurship and technology are not disposable in another country. The conventional theory implies that through foreign production they can reduce the cost per unit of their input factors, or create a greater value per unit cost.

MNCs benefit from overcoming and exploiting international market failures. This is known as the internalization of (foreign) markets. When the benefits from internalizing foreign markets are larger than the transaction costs in the external market systems, firms will choose to directly internalize markets rather than choose external market transactions.

Yet, there are other costs and risks attached to FDI. Because MNCs are less familiar with foreign business environment, government regulations, or local information than the local firms, MNCs must have critical advantageous assets to compensate for such foreignness. Such assets are referred to as monopolistic assets or ownership advantages (see Chapter 3). This perspective was largely supported by industrial organizational theorists in the 1970s with the rising view that the neoclassical trade theories have limitations in explaining new world trade patterns after the World War II (Smit, 2010).

Thus, FDI studies started from the assumptions of mobilizing resources across countries. The competitiveness of MNCs arise not from factor endowments but rather from tacitness or complexity of resources that cannot be easily imitated by others. Labor productivity is not the central issue in FDI studies as is in the trade theories. Workers are mobilized according to manager's decree. Rather, it is the managerial capability to utilize and mobilize the resources across countries to fully exploit the advantages from FDI.

Then why would a host country allow MNCs to exploit their rents from their national ground? The host country can utilize new foreign resources to upgrade and change its domestic industry structure. For example, a local worker employed and trained in the MNC can be transferred to a local firm or start up his (her) own company. Local firms working with the MNCs will also learn technologies and entrepreneurial skills by cooperating with them. Sometimes, MNC's presence heightens competition and motivates local firms to develop faster to survive. Growing competencies of local firms will then create local demands which in turn will become the driving force for further development of firms and local economy.

Thus, FDI theories can not only explain why countries grow fast, but also how industrial change takes place and some countries outperforme the originally more competitive ones. Yet, FDI study should be understood in complementary with trade theories by including foreign resources in the productivity equation. Trade balance does not represent only the local national wealth; exports are largely driven by MNCs. As a result, national competitiveness emanates from both domestic and foreign resources that are mobilized by MNCs, and firm competitiveness arises from efficient utilization of resources and talents around the globe.

2.2. Determinants of National Competitiveness

Trade and FDI have been the major means to gain and enhance sources of competitive advantage of nations and firms. Trade and FDI are tools of enhancing competitiveness, but we also need to know more fundamental sources of competitiveness. Porter (1990) explained that competitive advantage of nations arises from the interplay of four self-reinforcing determinants of diamond model which are: 1) factor conditions, 2) demand conditions, 3) firm strategy, structure and rivalry, 4) and related and supporting industries.

Factor conditions refer to factor inputs that are composed of production such as human and physical resources as well as infrastructure that are necessary to compete in a given industry. These factors are upgraded and changed through reinvestments. Demand conditions refer to the nature of home market demand for the industry's product or service. This can be divided into the size and the sophistication of market. Firm strategy, structure, and rivalry refer to both macro and micro conditions. The macro is the regulations and governance on how firms are created, organized, and managed, and the micro is the nature of industry structure that shapes the domestic rivalry. Porter (1990) explained that in the end the rivalry of the firm becomes the core in which the clustered firms can stimulate productivity and promote value creation that is the basis of national growth. Lastly, related and supporting industries refer to the presence of supplier industries and other related industries that are internationally competitive. Competitive supplier industries will reinforce innovation and internationalization in industries at later stages in the value system, whereas lack of competition and support industries often limits the (potential) productivity growth.[3]

Other than the four factors, Porter (1990) pointed out two exogenous variables, which are the government and chance events. The government factor includes incentives and regulations as well as other economic and industrial policies. Chance events include war, natural disaster, major technological breakthroughs, and other unexpected changes that disrupt the business environment. These two exogenous factors are considered not controllable by the firms in the industry, although they may affect the competitiveness of an industry or a nation.

The concept of diamond model gives multi-level implications in analyzing the competitiveness of nations, industries, and firms. Yet, the analysis is largely limited for two reasons. First, the model is based on the domestic realm which does not extend much beyond the trade theories. Porter

---

[3] The concept of external economies can be traced back to Marshall's work in 1920 and Graham's study in 1923 who were both preoccupied with the benefits of industrial districts which allow labor market pooling and knowledge spillover (Smit, 2010). Geographical proximity among concentrated firms promotes firm interactions and firms can benefit from information flow or monitoring competitors' strategic positions.

(1990) underestimated the value-added activities coming from foreign sources or the activities of MNCs. This is why Porter (1986, 1990) came to a conclusion that the most effective global strategy is to concentrate as many activities as possible in one country and serve the world from the home base, which misses out the important role of FDI for economic development (Moon, Rugman, and Verbeke, 1998). Porter (1990) focused on the superiority of the domestic factors and neglected the efficient combination of resources from home and foreign countries.

Second, sustainability is considered to come from the "advanced" factors of each determinant. For example, superior resources such as technology or the sophistication of the local market determine competitiveness of a nation. Yet it does not have to be always the superior technology to create national competitiveness. Rather, a good combination of foreign resources with the domestic ones allows an efficient creation of competitive advantages.

In order to solve these problems, Moon, Rugman, and Verbeke (1995) introduced generalized double diamond (GDD) model, which is an extended version of Porter's single diamond. Competitiveness should include international transactions of final and intermediary goods through trade (demand conditions) and of input factors such as human capital and technology through FDI (factor conditions). Furthermore, firm strategy, structure, and rivalry need to be considered in international realm. Firms compete globally and their strategies are shaped by the global competitors. The related and supporting sectors also need to be globally competitive and connected. The cluster of firms or firm networks should stretch beyond national boundaries to more effectively promote innovative interactions of firms. Thus in GDD model, internationalization of all four determinants of the diamond model is incorporated as illustrated in Figure 2.1.

The outer dashed-line diamond represents the total (domestic and international) competitiveness of a nation, while the inner solid-line diamond represents the domestic competitiveness. The diamond can vary in terms of size and shape depending on how much big or advanced each determinant is. The area between the two diamonds represents the degree of internationalization that is the value-added activities through internationalization.

Figure 2.1 shows the different shapes and sizes of two diamonds of South Korea and Singapore. As national competitiveness is measured in a

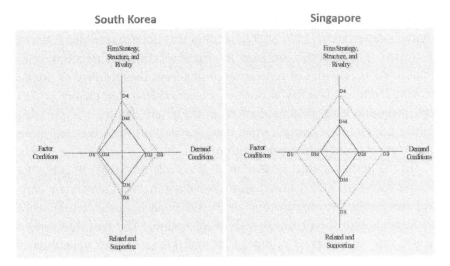

Figure 2.1   GDD Model of South Korea and Singapore
Source: Moon, Rugman, and Verbeke (1998).

relative sense, we can see that the domestic diamond of South Korea is bigger than that of Singapore but because of less internationalization, the overall competitiveness (outer diamond) is smaller than that of Singapore. Also, South Korea is skewed in factor conditions, which means that its international factor conditions are relatively less competitive than those of Singapore.

Then what is the key to enhancing national, industrial, and firm competitiveness? It is through finding a balanced combination of international and domestic competitive advantages, by complementing the disadvantages and imbalances in the diamond. Such efficient implementation in each area requires the encouragement of multinational activities so that MNCs have become the most effective driver through balancing out any disequilibrium in the diamond (see Chapter 4). Then, let us examine the theoretical background of internationalization and competitiveness more in detail.

2.3. Economic Perspectives

Stephan Hymer, the grandfather of FDI studies, first escaped from the general view on trade and financial theories, and analyzed MNCs from industrial organization perspective (Dunning and Rugman, 1985). Until Hymer's dissertation (1976 [1960]), economists did not consider FDI as a distinctive phenomenon because international firm transactions were considered as activities of generating profits from the arbitrage of capital moving from one country to another (Teece, 1986a). Yet, Hymer (1976) gave profound insights to the current world system that there is a market failure that some resources, other than capital, can also become more potent abroad and reduce competition.

In the perfect market system, there is no role for MNCs to play. The unique feature of FDI is a mechanism by which the MNCs maintain control over productive activities outside their national boundary and transfer resources within the firm across different nations. The rent that can be reaped from the arbitrage of input factor market gets bigger when there is a higher market failure. Hymer (1976) described market failure in factor and goods markets, but he did not recognize other types of market failure.

Calvet (1981), in an attempt to shift the perspective from the perfect market system to imperfect market system, specified four classes of market imperfections based on Kindleberger (1969): 1) market disequilibrium hypothesis, 2) government imposed distortions, 3) market structure imperfections, and 4) transaction cost-based market failure.[4] Let us take a look at each of them and see how they have paved a path for internalization theory.

2.3.1. *Market Disequilibrium Hypothesis*

The notion of perfect market system starts with price equilibrium, meaning prices are the same everywhere. In reality, however, there is disequilibrium in factor markets and foreign exchange markets (e.g., currency overvaluation). Such differences across countries create opportunities for profit-making by holding assets in undervalued currencies (Calvet, 1981). They will invest in assets and make profits until the market system makes the prices equalized across nations.

---

[4]Calvet (1981) called this type as the "market failure imperfections". Yet, as market failure has been used for structural market failure, we changed the terminology to transaction cost-based market failure.

Similar to capital and security markets, firms invest in low input-cost areas (e.g., labor costs) and they will invest until the prices become the same. This however means that as the price reaches the rate of equilibrium, foreign investors will sell assets, pocket the capital gain, and return to home operations. This means that FDI will cease eventually after the market reaches the equilibrium (Calvet, 1981).

2.3.2. *Government-Imposed Market Distortions*

If there were external factors such as the government that can manipulate and make distorted equilibrium or nullify the incentive for direct investment, price equilibrium or market disequilibrium hypothesis will not be enough to explain the causes of FDI. Tariffs and other non-tariff barriers are considered as FDI drivers, mainly imposed by the government. An increase in import barriers in export-target country may induce firms to be directly engaged in production to sell their products there than to produce domestically and export to that market. Tax policy also gives firms an incentive to invest in foreign countries as they will benefit more from production in a country with high tax reductions.

Market disequilibrium hypothesis and government-imposed market distortions are based on a relatively competitive market system. The former assumes that the market will come back to the equilibrium status over time, which means that the market mechanism still works. The latter assumes that the market is efficient enough to attract or woe foreign investors with exogenous incentives.

Yet, there are two cases where market is not competitive: 1) market structure imperfections, and 2) transaction cost-based imperfections. These two types have become the basis of market failure.

2.3.3. *Market Structure Imperfections*

In market structure imperfections, characterized as monopolistic or oligopolistic markets, there is a high entry barrier to prevent further competition. In this case, firms with competitive assets will invest abroad to generate rents. The more they invest, the bigger they will grow. As long as they can maintain monopolistic advantages in the imperfect market, MNCs will not only expand geographically, but they would also expand and diversify to other industries, and generate monopolistic rents.

The market structure failure from the monopolistic behaviors of MNCs became the foundation to Hymer's study. Hymer (1976) saw that MNCs invest abroad and transfer input factors in order to monopolize foreign markets. Because MNCs have resources that are not available in host countries, they generate additional rents by investing abroad. These resources can override any additional costs coming from "foreignness" so they are referred to as monopolistic assets. The result of this investment behavior is that the more MNCs expand, there will be more market failure. This is why Hymer asserted that MNCs should be regulated or prohibited from growing.

2.3.4. *Transaction Cost-Based Imperfections*

Transaction cost-based market imperfections regard that the market failure is endemic or natural. The market cannot be perfect from inefficient resource allocation due to external effects. Under this situation, firms look for two objectives: to provide channels for transferring knowledge at a lower cost and to slow down dissipation of knowledge to competitors. The former is done by lowering the transaction cost and the second is by internalizing (foreign) markets (see Section 2.3.5).

Transaction-cost theory looks into how firms economize the costs of business transactions over time. Transactions are largely defined by the nature of governance structure, yet without such governance, each transacting party will have, although they will seek a long-term interest to make both parties better off, an interest in selfishly appropriating as much of the gain as possible (Teece, 1986a). This is referred to as the opportunistic behavior of market participants. Market participants will also make "rational" decisions based on the information that is only available to them. This is referred to as bounded rationality. Because the market cannot control opportunistic behavior of participants as well as their accessible level of information, there always exists uncertainty in market transactions.

Particularly, when the transactions are made abroad or with unfamiliar parties, the transaction costs coming from attaining information, bargaining, and enforcing transactions tend to rise. Thus making interactions internally (i.e., through standardized systems) can become more efficient. This is why Williamson (1981) dichotomized market from the firm (hierarchy). A firm can develop governance structure or a hierarchy to minimize opportunism. In the external market, on the other hand, there is no governance structure (no control and management) so that transactions are freely made between sellers and buyers. Thus, firms try to "internalize market" to shield transactions and minimize market failure or transaction costs by setting a governance system.[5]

2.3.5. *Internalization Theory*

Internalization theory dates back to Coase (1937) who recognized that costs occur in market transactions, so firms try to internalize to make transactions more efficient (Moon, 2004b). Internalization is extended from the transaction-cost analysis, but it can also be extended to explain the structural market failure. Even if the firm wants to sell its monopolistic assets, the value of such assets may not be as valuable or may be underestimated in other countries. This means that there is no appropriate market to make transactions at the expected level of value. Thus, firms will instead set internal prices (Moon, 2004b).

Whereas the traditional economics regarded information/knowledge as a public resource, it was Buckley and Casson (1976) who first made a linkage between the knowledge market imperfections and internalization as a paradigm for FDI theories. Because some knowledge is embodied only in few firms, knowledge is considered as scarce or valuable. Firms with valuable knowledge can invest abroad to appropriate rents. On the other hand, certain knowledge is embedded in specific locations which attract firm's investment to internalize the location-specific knowledge. This is a step to move from the analysis of one particular imperfection toward the development of a more general theory of FDI.

---

[5] Williamson (1975) explained that because of bounded rationality, opportunism, and asset specificity, transactions costs arise from information costs, bargaining costs, and enforcement costs.

In this case, there are two ways that firms can internalize external markets or appropriate external transactions. One is horizontal integration and the other is vertical integration. The vertical integration occurs when the transactions of inputs/outputs are internalized within a firm. Horizontal integration occurs when the transaction of different lines of goods is internalized. Then, why would a firm try to internalize the markets when they could let others do the job (externalization)?

If there are two firms, one producing a mobile phone and the other a computer, and the mobile phone producer sells its technology to the computer producer, there arises an issue of how much information to reveal. If the firm opens up too much about the technology, it is transferring the knowledge for (almost) free so that it loses the chance to appropriate rents from selling it. If it does not open up enough, then there occurs information asymmetry and the buyer will not be able to see whether the technology is worth buying or not.

If there is no effective regime or mechanism that can solve this problem, the issue of transferring knowledge lies in firm's teaching and learning ability. If the mobile phone producer wants to license its technology to a computer producer which does not have the ability to learn fast or is not competent to exploit the newly adopted technology, then the mobile phone business cannot be able to fully appropriate rents of the technology. On the other hand, if the technology is too complicated to teach the licensee, then there needs repeated transfer of knowledge which increases the costs. Firms will then choose to internalize the market through integrating horizontally.

The same logic can be applied to vertical integration as well. A mobile phone firm may develop a new technology for its new product and ask the supplier to upgrade its parts and components. If the supplier does not have the ability to absorb and incorporate the technology to its business, then the mobile phone firm will not be able to appropriate full rents from its new technological development. Then, the firm would internalize backward activities, and establish vertical integration to minimize the transaction expenses that would have derived from repeated communication.

Also, if there is only one supplier to provide parts and components for the mobile phone producer, then the mobile phone firm has to be totally dependent on the supplier. Yet, the supplier can take an opportunistic behavior to either lower the quality or increase the price to exploit more rents. In order to leverage the power over the supplier, it is better for a firm to make an investment to have a certain level of control over the supplier, meaning it will, to a various degree, internalize the related activities. Full internalization of the market can be done through setting up a wholly-owned subsidiary or mergers and acquisitions (M&A). On the other hand, only a certain level of internalization can be done through forming a strategic alliance or a joint venture, where the control of the assets is limited to its investment ratio (see Chapter 8).

2.3.6. *Market Imperfections as Foundations to FDI*

The two market failures, structural and transaction cost based, became the basis of the FDI theories, which was a big shift from trade theories based on perfect market system. Market structure imperfection was developed based on Bain's (1956) work and has become the basis of Hymer's (1976) dissertation.[6] It is known as Hymer's Bain type of market imperfections. On the other hand, transaction-cost imperfection is based on Coase's (1937) or Williamson's (1975) transaction theory.

These two types of market imperfections, Hymer-type and Williamson-type, are often misunderstood. They are not only complicated but are used in many studies without clear distinctions. Yet, the distinction between the two comes down to either endogenous or exogenous pressures. In the case of Hymer-type of structural imperfections,[7] the pressure emanates endogenously for the firm to grow larger particularly in the international market. Whereas in the case of Williamson-type of market failure, firms need to overcome exogenous risks and costs associated with foreignness, so that they need to internalize external/foreign markets to make transfer of resources more efficient.

---

[6] Market structure imperfections come from economies of scale, knowledge advantages, distribution networks, product diversification, and credit advantages.

[7] As an extension to Coasian theory about why firms form vertical integration, Hymer (1976) explained vertical integration of MNCs by four criteria: Reduction of internal conflict, uncertainty of markets, imperfection of financial markets and insufficiency of relevant information (Horaguchi and Toyne, 1990).

This is why the two views of market imperfection take different perspectives on MNCs. The scholars of structural market failure see that as MNCs bulk up their size to exploit their monopolistic advantages, they remove competition and deteriorate market imperfections. Thus, MNCs were regarded to be negative and need to be regulated (Dunning and Rugman, 1985). On the other hand, transaction cost-based scholars see that MNCs make markets more efficient so need to be promoted rather than. In this respect, Rugman (1981) stated that MNCs are both the victim of and villain for the market imperfections. At the initial stage, MNCs will emerge as a victim to reduce transaction costs in the market, but as they become big, they will grow to become the villain which will continuously take advantage of their monopolistic power in the market.

Although the earlier studies on trade and FDI were couched within the framework of existing mainstream economics, they have evolved to link economic perspective with business studies toward a "management-flavored discipline" (Narula, 2010). In current parlance, the costs of technology transfer lie in the degree of "tacitness or complexity" of knowledge (Kogut and Zander, 1992) which requires a special set of managerial skills to efficiently allocate and transfer them between firms. This can be also referred to as the intangible business assets. Thus, along with the cost-based economic perspective on FDI, business perspectives give us a more comprehensive and in-depth understanding of FDI.

2.4. Business Perspectives

The heterogeneity and asymmetrical distribution of managerial assets have become crucial as they evolve over time and create unique advantages of a firm (Horaguchi and Toyne, 1990). This can create new markets by providing new products, organizations, management techniques, and technologies which cannot be explained by transaction cost theories — a lower transaction cost does not create a larger market.

There are three kinds of resources that are available to firms. The first is the (public) resources that are assumed to be available to every firm. The second type is the resources that are internally built by the firm, such as organizational skills and tacit knowledge. The third type of resources is the firm network-based advantages. The advantages arise not exclusively outside of the firm boundary nor internally, but in the firm networks. Firms build resources together or generate advantages such as barriers to entry or knowledge channel to external information which is crucial in dealing with external market changes and creating new knowledge.

Among these three types of resources, the latter two are the created assets that are hard to be replicated by others. They are either technically difficult to imitate or are legally protected. The proprietary use of the resources allows firms to monopolize and generate rents from them. In these cases, it is not a matter of accessibility, but a matter of difficulty to be imitated or transferred to others. Simply put, the economic perspective is a point of accessibility to the resources, whereas business perspective is about the creation of scarce and valuable resources.

Business scholars have looked into what makes firms competitive. Here, we are going to look at two kinds of resources (firm-specific resources and network resources) that contribute to the competitiveness of a firm. The firm-specific studies view that the resources are embodied in the firm, and this stream is called the resource-based view. The network-specific studies view that the competitive advantage is embedded in firm networks and this stream is called the network-based or relational view. We will examine these two views and other related perspectives more closely in the following sections.

2.4.1. *Resource-Based View (Static View)*

Resource-based view of the firm perceives that in order for firms to reduce competition, firms need to find heterogeneous and immobile resources to target untapped markets. This aligns with the concept of Hymer's monopolistic rents. Barney (1991) who has theorized the resource-based view of the firm explained that firms need to actively seek and create resources that are valuable, rare, inimitable, and non-substitutable. The resources are broadly categorized as three: 1) physical capital resources, 2) human capital resources, and 3) organizational capital resources.

Physical capital resources refer to technologies, firm's equipment and plants, and its access to raw materials that allow firms to create value-added products. Human capital resources refer to training, experience, judgment, intelligence, and insights of individual managers and workers of the firm. Specific kinds of managerial expertise are also included in this category.[8] Organizational capital resources include firm's structure, culture, routine, informal planning, coordinating and controlling systems as well as informal relations among groups within a firm and those in its environment (Barney, 1991). Firm's particular routines and organizational structure mobilize both the physical and human capital resources (Nelson and Winter, 1982). At first, scholars focused on innovation and knowledge-based assets as the core competence of the firm (e.g., Bartlett and Ghoshal, 1989; Prahalad and Doz, 1987) but it was later evolved to incorporate a broader scope of variables, such as the governance structure.

Yet, the resource-based view of the firm is largely criticized for being "static". For example, a newly developed technology may be valuable and rare at a certain point, but it can be substituted any time by other technologies and lose its competitive position, regardless of legal protective measures of the technology. A shift from analogue technology to digital technology is a good example. Thus, scholars started shifting their view on heterogeneous and immobile resources to the firm capabilities to adapt to changing environments. Rather than saying a certain superior technology is the source of competitive advantage (this is limited to a certain time frame), the ability to continuously develop superior technologies became the core aspect of creating competitive advantage. The dynamic capability has thus evolved as an extended theory to the resource-based view of the firm.

2.4.2. *Learning Capability (Dynamic View)*

In fast changing and knowledge-intensive business landscapes, competitiveness is derived from firms' capability of learning, or absorbing and

---

[8] The managerial resources that sustain competitive advantage include "all assets, capabilities, organizational processes, firm attributes, information, and knowledge, controlled by a firm that enable the firm to conceive or implement strategies that improve its efficiency and effectiveness" (Barney, 1991:101).

creating new knowledge. As resource-based view remains static, other scholars have the evolutionary and dynamic perspectives on firm competitiveness. The static view cannot explain why some firms have competitive advantages in rapid, unpredictable, and changing environment and how they evolve through time (Eisenhardt and Martin, 2000). Thus, scholars have shifted from "what" resources to "how" factors in searching for the competitive sources of the firm.

Dynamic Capability[9]

Dynamic capability is defined as the ability to integrate, build, and reconfigure internal and external competencies to address rapidly changing environments (Teece, Pisano, and Shuen, 1997) or to match and even create market change (Eisendhardt and Martin, 2000). There are variations in defining dynamic capability, yet they share common features of reorganizing, modifying, and creating resource bases to renew the current resources (e.g., Zollo and Winter, 2002; Winter, 2003).

Dynamic capability is not something that could be bought; it is built through a long period of time internally. The evolution of such capability is embodied in a routine or in firm's process or mechanism to better manage and deal with external market changes. It is also embedded in the ability of managers and employees. They may be idiosyncratic to each firm (Teece, Pisano, and Shuen, 1997) or there could be commonalities or routines of best practice among firms (Eisenhardt and Martin, 2000).

Absorptive Capacity

If dynamic capability is about adaptation to the external environment, gaining new external knowledge is called as the absorptive capacity. There are variations in defining absorptive capacity but the fundamental comes

---

[9] This was disaggregated to three stages by Teece (2007): 1) sensing and shaping opportunities and threats, 2) seizing opportunities, and 3) maintaining competitiveness through enhancing, combining, protecting, and reconfiguring the business enterprises' tangible and intangible assets.

down to the organizational learning process of accumulating and exploiting new knowledge.[10]

Then, what helps firms learn better and faster? Some scholars pointed the prior existing knowledge or learning before doing (Cohen and Levinthal, 1990; Pisano, 1994). Among the existing knowledge, complementary knowledge is likely to be transformed or exploited by the firm more easily than dissimilar knowledge (Zahra and George, 2002). Motivation is also a trigger to enhance absorptive capacity (Minbaeva et al., 2003). The more willingness the workers have in learning or transferring, the more knowledge will be exchanged.

Combinative Capabilities

Since Schumpeter (1934: 66) noted "The development in our sense is defined by carrying out new combinations", many scholars have shown that a new resource combination is a source of innovation (e.g., Koruna, 2004). Firms could either reconfigure existing resources or combine with new external knowledge. The external knowledge is attained from consumer markets, the location (clustered firms) or firm networks. The essence of combinative capability is to create value from reconfiguring and recombining resource stocks and knowledge (Kogut and Zander, 1992).

The appropriate level of combination is crucial. Diversity enhances learning capability of the firm and serves as a source of innovation (March, 1991). Yet, too much diversified knowledge can limit the capacity building whereas narrowly focused knowledge inhibits firms to capture opportunities or put firms into a trap of "path-dependency". Also, if firms merge too often with other firms in order to gain new knowledge stocks, managers cannot learn appropriate lessons of any particular acquisition while too few acquisitions in a long period of time can make managers not have enough opportunities to hone their skills (Eisenhardt and Martin, 2000).

---

[10] All these are assumed under the effective appropriability regime. In low efficacy of intellectual property rights and ease of replication, firms fail to appropriate the returns to their new knowledge creation work (Teece, 1986b).

Along the dynamic perspective line, absorptive capacity is focused on identifying and attaining new knowledge source, while combinative capability is focused on combining and transforming the resources. Their roles overlap to some extent but they together become the basis of firms' capability to adapt to the changing environments.

2.5. Network and Relational View

A good resource portfolio is formed through inter-firm relationships. Prior studies have looked for sources of competitive advantages within the boundary of an individual firm (Porter, 2000b). Yet, no firms can survive alone. Firms cooperate together to generate new knowledge.

Inter-firm relationships do not necessarily mean direct relationships that are formed deliberately. Firm networks can be indirectly built from situating physically close to each other. Firms that are situated geographically close to each other are referred to as clusters (Krugman, 1991a; Porter, 1998a). Firms can benefit from a better access to employees and suppliers, access to specialized information, the quality and efficiency of complementarities such as hotels, restaurants, shopping outlets, and transportation facilities (Porter, 1998a). Peer pressures from other firms in clusters also motivate firms to compete and innovate, which in turn create self-reinforcing mechanisms for further development and spillover effects.

This is why firms try to situate themselves in the hub of knowledge flow either physically or virtually. Physical hub, meaning clusters, is where knowledge and resources are concentrated in a specific region. Virtual hub, although they may not be physically clustered together, is a network of firms, universities, and other institutions that facilitate diverse knowledge exchange. In order to have access to those networks, firms need to form relationships with the firms that broker other networks.

Inter-firm networks are defined by their intensity of relationships, strong or weak. Strong relationships tend to be formed over time, or they are built through extensive engagement. On the other hand, weak relationships are built over a short period of time, or entail less frequent interactions of firms. It is important to distinguish these two types of relationships because if the knowledge a firm intends to transfer is hard to be codified, it can be more efficiently transferred in strong relationships. On the other hand, explicit knowledge can be readily transferred in weak relationships.

From the social perspective, competitive routines or mechanisms are referred to as social capital. Social capital has its roots in interpersonal relationships, which have been applied to intra- and inter-organizational relationships. Some scholars have espoused a broader definition of social capital to include social norms and values (e.g., Portes and Sensenbrenner, 1993) as well as common codes and visions shared within the firm and among collaborating firms (e.g., Tsai and Ghoshal, 1998). Social capital or the relational resource serves as a channel for information and resource flows (Tsai and Ghoshal, 1998) and creates values higher than the ones that can be created by individual firms alone. More active interactions among business units and firms stimulate the formation of common interests and induce a higher level of innovation (Gabbay and Zuckerman, 1998). Social capital also strengthens supplier relationships, regional production networks, and inter-firm learning (Adler and Kwon, 2002; Uzzi, 1997; Romo and Schwartz, 1995; Kraatz, 1998).

2.6. Institutional View

Business studies have regarded institutions as a mere "background" to firms' performance and competition when analyzing firm competitive advantages (Peng, Wang, and Jiang, 2008). Yet institutions make a critical part of firm performance. The formal institutions refer to policies, law, rules, and regulations that affect firm strategies. Informal institutions are moderated by norms, cognitions, and culture that underpin formal institutions (Redding, 2005; Hofstede, 2007). Both formal and informal institutions are referred to as the "rules of the game" that structure firm interactions (North, 1990).

Formal institutions are like antitrust law enforced in the US whereas they are not enforced in China. In China, corporate executives at competing firms can legally sit down to discuss pricing and carve up markets whereas such practice has been labeled as illegal and been outlawed for more than 100 years in the US market under the antitrust law (Peng, Wang and Jiang, 2008). Even if the Chinese firms have been competitive in production and servicing customers, it would have been convicted as collusion if they approached their business activities of the Chinese style in the US.

Informal institutions are like "guanxi" in China, which means (interpersonal) network system. Without building guanxi with the "right" people in China, it is difficult to do business even with competitive resources and capabilities. Thus, firms that may not try to build personal relationships in other nations may have to form guanxi when doing business in China (Li, 2005; Xu, et al., 2006).

Institutions vary across industries, countries, and regions and they interact in various ways. Without understanding such different institutional forms of corporations among countries, firms may make corporate governance (reform) policies irrelevant, counterproductive, and in the worst case a failure (Peng, Wang and Jiang, 2008). Thus, it is important to understand the international rule of game that may be different from that at home.

2.7. Conclusion

This chapter examines the means of internationalization and competitiveness as well as theoretical background from economic and business perspectives that explain the sources of competitive advantage. The conventional perspective of competitive advantage, particularly trade theories, starts from two assumptions. The first is that the competitive advantage is confined to the national boundary. The second is that the sources of competitive advantage need to be "superior" to those embedded in other locations.

Based on these assumptions, the economic perspective sees that MNCs economize information to overcome market failure (Rugman, 1980) or seek rents from lower transaction costs (Hennart, 1982; Arrow, 1974) that may arise from physical and psychic distances (economic, social, and linguistic dissimilarities between regions) (Kogut and Zander, 1993). In business perspective, MNCs exist because of the desire to create and capture values (Pitelis and Teece, 2010). Firms do so to exploit existing competitive advantage or to create new sources of competitive advantage.

We have examined several important studies of competitiveness in which most of them are covered by a comprehensive framework of Porter's diamond model. According to the diamond model, the resource-based view mainly analyzes the factor conditions of the diamond, while the network or relational view analyzes the related and supporting sectors.

The institution-based view covers the (macro) business context as well as the government. Dynamic views, on the other hand, are related to changing market conditions, or the chance events. The diamond model is thus an excellent tool for integrating various perspectives of competitiveness, but still has a limitation in incorporating international source of competitiveness, which needs to be extended to GDD model. The GDD model explains how competitive advantages are developed by integrating foreign and domestic advantages through time.

Chapter 3

The Western Perspective on FDI: From Market Failure to OLI Paradigm

Summary

The most popular Foreign Direct Investment (FDI) theory is the OLI paradigm, constructed by John H. Dunning. He introduced the OLI or eclectic paradigm that is composed of three variables: ownership advantage, location advantage, and internalization advantage. The ownership advantage is what makes firms invest abroad; location advantage is where such investments are made; and internalization advantage is how transactions are made. This paradigm is based on the developed country's perspective of exploiting monopolistic advantages that outweigh the costs arising from foreignness when doing business abroad. The OLI paradigm has advanced over the years to explain characteristics of multinational corporation (MNC) activities of a knowledge and value creator and has remained until today as a powerful framework for examining FDI.

3.1. Dunning's OLI Paradigm

John H. Dunning put forward the theory on FDI, based on Hymer's (1976 [1960]) dissertation which was the backbone of FDI studies (see Chapter 2). When Dunning first developed the eclectic paradigm during the mid-1950s and presented it at a Nobel Symposium in Stockholm in 1976, he would not have guessed that the paradigm would turn out to be eclectic. During these times, the US firms were investing outside of their self-sufficient economy to explore new markets mainly in Europe. There arose a question then why competitive US firms would invest abroad, instead of trading the final goods. Why did these firms choose to produce in Europe than domestically?

After the World War II, the US and the UK were the two leading nations in the world economy. Yet, the US firms were on average two to five times more productive than their UK counterparts in the manufacturing sector (Dunning, 2001a). Dunning (1958) then questioned what made the US firms more productive than the UK firms. Was it the resource or the managerial capability that the firms had or was it the resource or system embedded in the home country (US)?

When we look back to traditional trade theories, production resources are bounded by national borders. All firms have equal access to all resources within a country so there was no distinction between the location resources and firm resources. However, in FDI studies, resources can be mobilized across national borders. Not all firms have equal access to the resources and some resources are confined to only a few firms. MNCs, by transferring such scarce resources across national borders, could benefit and create opportunities that outweigh the costs of doing business abroad. Some resources, on the other hand, are sticky to the location and cannot be transferred across national borders by MNCs. Sometimes, these sticky resources conversely attract MNCs' investments. Based on these assumptions, Dunning (1958) found that there were two kinds of resources, one is embedded in firms and the other in the location. Dunning (1958) called the former as the ownership advantage and the latter as the location advantage.

In order to find which resources made the US firms more productive than the UK firms, Dunning (1958) examined the US MNCs that invested in the UK. If the US affiliates performed as well as their parent companies at home, and fairly better than the UK competitors, the resources are embedded in the parent firm and are likely to be transferred to their affiliates across national borders. If the US affiliates in the UK recorded no better performances than their parent company or UK competitors, the resources would be embedded in the US.

The result was that the US affiliates in the UK were not as productive as their parent companies but were more productive than the UK firms (Dunning, 1958; 2001a). Dunning interpreted that this result of the US affiliates in the UK being less competitive than the parent company at home is because some of the domestic resources in the US are helping the

US firms to be more productive than the firms in the UK. At the same time, the US affiliates being more competitive compared to the UK firms is because of the ownership advantages that were transferred from the parent company. In other words, the productivity difference between the US MNCs and the UK firms could be explained partly by the ownership (O) advantage of the US firms and the location (L) advantages in the US. This finding to distinguish O advantage from L advantage was a significant contribution.

Then, why do firms opt to exploit their O advantages through internalization than sell or externalize them through international market system? Firms tend to establish their own subsidiaries and internalize their transactions abroad. Sometimes, they create rents from transactions in imperfect market systems. This advantage was later added and named as the internalization (I) advantage (Dunning, 1980; 1998).

The addition of I advantage explains how firms obtain and add new assets to their core competencies and protect their competitive position (Dunning, 2001a). Dunning explained that the benefit of FDI derives from O advantage, prior to I advantage. This means that firms invest abroad to exploit O advantage and I advantage arises from the way O advantage is exploited (Dunning, 2001a). In this way, O advantage, L advantage, and I advantage became the tripods of the OLI paradigm.

Over the years, the OLI paradigm has been revised in two aspects to better explain the changing patterns of MNC activities. First, it originated from Hymer's (1976) thesis on monopolistic rents and structural market failure, and has evolved to embrace transactional market failures and various business theories of the resource-based view, network-based, and institution-based view of the firm (see Chapter 2). Second, the theory started off as a static analysis of the initial FDI motivations but it was revised to include the dynamic aspect by giving more credit to managerial capabilities — allocating and augmenting resources abroad to enhance firm's competitive position.

Let us take a look at each pillar of the OLI paradigm which answers three questions as follows: 1) should a firm engage in foreign production? (O advantage), if yes, then 2) where should the firm invest? (L advantage), and 3) how should the firm invest, i.e., through internalization or arm's length arrangements (I advantage)?

3.1.1. *Ownership Advantage*

The most fundamental variable that constitutes the OLI paradigm is O advantage.[1] Firms that have monopolistic assets will invest abroad and benefit from setting barriers to entry and nullifying any disadvantages coming from foreignness (Bain, 1956; Porter, 1980; 1985). This was identified as the ownership asset (*Oa*) and refers to the property rights and intangible asset advantages that arise from the resource (asset) structure of the firm.[2] These resources have been built internally by a firm to match the existing market needs (Dunning, 2001a). In this respect, this view aligns with the resource-based view on firm resources. Assuming that resources are idiosyncratic and immobile, a firm can maximize rent creation by setting monopolistic strategy.[3]

This ownership asset is distinguished from firm's capability in coordinating resources in multiple locations and capturing gains from risk diversification (Dunning and Lundan, 2008a). Unlike *Oa*, this is related to the synergistic effects created from multi-nationality. By diversifying their investments in diverse countries, firms gain experiences and new knowledge sets about different business environments. Indeed, the economic rents are created from deploying and creating resources than from mere capital equipment and property. Firm's advantages of effectively allocating and coordinating resources in different locations under well-organized governance system are called transactional advantages (*Ot*). This aligns with the dynamic capability or managerial competencies of firms. Firms deploy and create new resources to enhance competitiveness across national borders by simultaneously increasing global integration and local responsiveness (e.g., Prahalad and Doz, 1987; Bartlett and Ghoshal, 1989).[4] Thus the focus of

---

[1] Dunning distinguished between the asset (*Oa*) and transaction (*Ot*) advantages of the MNCs which came after distinguishing the two types of market failures (structural and transaction cost market imperfections).

[2] The ownership asset is composed of product innovation, production management, organizational and marketing systems, innovatory capacity, non-codifiable knowledge, accumulated experience in marketing, finance, and the ability to reduce costs of intra- and/or inter-firm transactions (Dunning and Lundan, 2008a).

[3] The condition of the resources being monopolized by only a few firms is that such monopoly would not hurt the social welfare.

[4] Dynamic capability is the extension to the resource-based view (see Chapter 2).

O advantage shifted from internally developed resources to the capabilities to access and organize knowledge-intensive assets throughout the world and integrating them to firm's value chain activities with other firms (Dunning, 2000).[5]

Dunning explained that the most successful MNCs are those that are able to nurture and exploit both *Oa* and *Ot* advantages. With regard to firm cooperation, however, Dunning added a new aspect of institutional assets (*Oi*). *Oi* is the capability of the firm to ally with other firms to further strengthen its core assets and cover the range of formal and informal institutions that govern the value-added process of the firm, and between the firm and its stakeholders (Dunning and Lundan, 2008b). It can also be understood in terms of intangible resources such as routines, values, and enforcement mechanisms labeled as the corporate culture that determine the conduct of firm activities.

In short, ownership advantages have been evolved from economic to managerial assets, from static resources to dynamic capabilities. In addition, O advantages are not only built internally but are co-developed with other cooperating and complementing firms throughout the world. Therefore, MNCs do not just choose or prefer one specific kind of resource over the other. The different kinds of O advantages allow firms to outperform their rivals in the host country.

3.1.2. *Location Advantage*

In the traditional trade and investment theories, there were no clear distinctions between resources that are embedded in the firm and resources in the location. Yet, from the 1960s, location factors and spatial concentration or diversification started to gain attention in terms of how they affect the competitiveness of investing firms. Rugman (1979) averred that other than having the resources that may be directly embedded in the location, having the investment diversified across regions can also reduce and diversify risks for MNCs. Other scholars stressed that firms can complement their advantages through augmenting activities and promoting cooperation with other firms in innovation, production,

---

[5] This was later extended to alliance capitalism.

and marketing (e.g., Teece, 1992; Dunning, 2000). In this respect, L advantages, marked off from the O advantages, became an important factor for the location and timing of MNCs' overseas investment (e.g., Cushman, 1985).

Traditional location-specific resources such as natural resources, cheap and large labor pool, and market size are exploited by the MNCs. Yet, these location assets are not sustainable and their values deplete over time. Rather what makes a location attractive is the created assets that are specifically bounded by clusters of firms and are not readily replicable by other countries (Porter, 1998b). The mechanism that facilitates knowledge of cluster exchanges sustains and creates value which is also referred to as social capital.

The value-creating networks include inter-linkages with universities and other institutions. When firms and institutions have close ties, they exchange and create new knowledge. The newly added knowledge fosters innovation and enhances the learning capacity of firms. By having such advantages that last long and are unique among other potentially competing firms, the country can attract MNCs and remain competitive over other rival countries. L advantages can thus benefit both MNCs and the host country.

L advantages vary depending on institutional structures. They shape firm strategies, economic efficiency, growth, and social well-being (Dunning and Lundan, 2008b). For example, Japanese institutional features are different from the US and the Western Europe and thus contributed differently to the develoment of the Japanese economy between the mid-1980s and the mid-1990s. (Dunning and Lundan, 2008b; Florida and Kenny, 1994). This gives implications for policy-makers to foster a favorable business environment and provide an appropriate economic and social infrastructure that can attract and retain MNCs' value-added activities (Dunning, 2000).

Through the interactions among clustered firms and various institutions, firms augment new knowledge and build capabilities to the changing environments. Also by exchanging information, firms transform and adapt dynamically to the changing environments. Thus, the location factor becomes the source of competitiveness and "strategic trajectories" of the MNCs (Dunning, 2000).

In short, the focus of location-specific advantages has shifted from inherited tangible assets to created intangible assets, from disposal resources to sustainable location-bounded resources and from a simple location for exploiting O advantages to a competitive location for value-added activities of MNCs. The L advantage is thus not only about the production inputs but is also largely fashioned by the interactions between firm networks and relationships with institutions of the location.

3.1.3. *Internalization Advantage*

If firms have the advantages to go abroad and have chosen the location to invest, they need to decide how to invest. Dunning (1998; 2000) explained that the alternatives range from buying and selling goods in open market through a variety of non-equity agreements between firms, to the integration of intermediate product markets and an outright purchase of a foreign production (Dunning, 2000). The degree of control and ownership are explained by what we call as the entry modes (see Chapter 8). The lowest degree of the entry mode is licensing, having no control or ownership over the licensee. As the licensee activities have no direct relation to the operations of the licensing company, licensing is considered as externalization. On the other hand, a firm may want to have a certain level of control or ownership, through joint ventures or wholly owned subsidiary, which is called as internalization of foreign markets.

The entry mode to foreign country varies depending on the environmental context. Yet, the OLI paradigm avows that with greater net benefits of internalizing cross-border intermediate product markets, the more likely a firm will prefer to engage in foreign production, rather than giving rights to foreign producers or sellers through technical service or franchise agreements. The internalizing benefit increases from reducing costs coming from unnecessary transactions in the external market and increasing efficiency through intra-firm transactions. Thus, there exists I advantage as long as the transaction costs of using external arm's length markets in the exchange of, for example, intermediate products, information, technology, marketing techniques, exceed those incurred by internal hierarchies (Dunning, 2000).

We can see that this was added after acknowledging the costs not only coming from firm transactions but also from coordination and augmentation of new resources from the location. Having been influenced by the Scandinavian school on the learning perspective, the Uppsala Model, these features reflect the dynamic perspective of firm's engagement in foreign productions over a long run, and provide solutions to overcome the criticisms for analyzing FDI motivations from a static perspective in the past.

However, there were criticisms on Dunning's I advantage. It is very limited and there are other functions which a firm may perform in foreign countries. For example, a firm may seek internalizing foreign markets in order to forestall or thwart the behavior of competitors (Dunning, 2000). In practice, firms do not always submissively react to market failures. They have more proactive attitude toward searching for and complementing new resources. They recognize, integrate, and reconfigure their resources and capabilities to find efficiencies in their value chain activities. This shows how Dunning's I advantage has been widened to incorporate all costs associated with any value-added activities from a mere transaction cost analysis.

Thus, Dunning's last ladder of the OLI paradigm shifted from internalization theory to reducing transaction and coordination cost, and to business perspectives on managerial discretion to complement and augment assets. This is not to submissively react to the changing environments but to proactively enhance the firm's O advantages by combining them with L advantages. Whereas the asset augmentation was conventionally considered to be done by an individual firm, I advantage lies in the interaction between firm networks and institutions. The degree of internalization (e.g., control and ownership over local firms and institutions) varies depending on the cost-benefit analysis within the macroeconomic environment of uncertainty and volatility (see Chapter 7).

This shows that as the OLI tripod has evolved, each of the factors has become not mutually exclusive (Dunning, 2000). Although Dunning remained at the conventional aspect of advantages in explaining the theory, the new modified modality has given significant implications for further research. Particularly, the last component of the OLI paradigm has helped the FDI studies embrace alliance-related and asset-augmenting MNC activities.

3.2. Analysis and Extension of the Eclectic (OLI) Paradigm

3.2.1. *Independent or Inter-dependent?*

So far, we have delved into the tripods of OLI paradigm. For modeling a paradigm, we have to search for all important variables that are mutually exclusive. We call this "No missing, no overlapping". If we are asked whether OLI variables are independent, it is hard to draw a clear line among them. For example, O advantage and I advantage have both evolved to incorporate managerial capability for asset augmentation. Thus, rather than trying to clarify their specificity, we can distinguish them based on "where" the advantages are embedded.

Yet, independent variables do not necessarily translate to strict independence of the variables; the tripods are built on their inter-dependent relationship. One variable has an influence on other variables. In addition, an exogenous variable, for example, will have an influence on a firm's ownership advantages and how a firm chooses and utilizes its advantages to internalize new resources. Overall, a change in one variable influences other variables over time, in which it becomes difficult to identify the separate identities of these variables (Dunning, 2001a). They are also highly contextual. The advantages generate rents differently based on their contextual settings. For example, they vary depending on the economic and political features of the host country, or the nature of the firm and industry.

Although it may be difficult to generalize across industries, we can infer that the more favorable configuration of OLI they have, the more the firms are likely to engage in FDI. For example, pharmaceutical companies will engage in foreign production more than firms in iron industries because the pharmaceutical companies will generate more unique ownership advantages and benefit more from internalizing cross-border intermediate product markets (Dunning, 2000). This applies the same to the relationship between large and small firms. Large firms tend to have greater ownership advantages than the small firms, so they will find more reasons to invest abroad.

3.2.2. *OLI Paradigm, Alliance Capitalism and Institutional View*

The conventional analysis on firm competitiveness and FDI was confined to an individual firm level. Yet, as the economy has become increasingly inter-dependent, it is almost impossible to analyze FDI without considering firm networks and the business context in which firms operate. In fact, firms outside of the US evolved from extensive inter-firm linkages, for example, the *keiretsu* in Japan and the *chaebol* in Korea. Thus, Dunning incorporated the concept of alliance capitalism in 1997, following Gerlarch's (1992) work on social organization of Japanese keiretsu (Dunning, 1997). To understand the unique features of alliance capitalism, it is crucial to examine how prior studies, arm's length capitalism and hierarchical capitalism, perceive firm alliances.

The arm's length capitalism[6] is similar to neoclassical economics that all transaction costs are zero and are determined by market forces only. This means that market participants buy and sell their inputs and outputs at fair prices in arm's length market. Thus, firm cooperation is considered to be a symptom of structural market failure; a means to enhance the monopolistic position in the market (Colombo, 1998).

Yet, with input resources being mobilized by FDI and other modes of cross-border entrepreneurial and asset transference, operation inefficiency can occur. In order to minimize transaction and coordination costs across nations, the trajectory of capitalism in the world economy has evolved to what is known as the hierarchical capitalism (Williamson, 1975, 1985).[7] This is to say that the governance of production and transactions is determined by the relative costs and benefits of using markets and firms as alternative organizational modes (Colombo, 1998). To coordinate these different activities, the administrative system takes on the guise of a hierarchy (Colombo, 1998).

Until the 1970s, firm cooperation was considered exceptional or alternative where the deployment of resources and capabilities in market oriented economy has been shaped by a micro-organizational system known

---

[6] Arm's length capitalism regards that there are no externalities of production or consumption.
[7] Hierarchical form of organization dominated from 1870s to 1980s (Dunning, 1997).

as hierarchical capitalism. Any kind of horizontal firm alliances were done based on contracts and were considered as a quasi-hierarchical capitalism. Until then, as firms make decisions under the bounded rationality and opportunism, they cooperate only to the extent that they can bear risks and costs of internalizing new resources.

The distinctive features of the firms from the past still persist but firm cooperation (even without equity investments) has started to become main constitutions in wealth creating process (Dunning, 1997). In other words, alliance capitalism was substituting arm's length market capitalism. Along the value-added chain, firms are engaging in both cooperation and competition with other firms and institutions. Firms ally not only to protect and exploit their capabilities but also to complement their assets and speed up their innovative and learning process.

Firms formed networks with the institutions and governments as they have increasingly shaped business environments to better utilize foreign resources and upgrade the quality of domestic ones in order to attain their economic goals. In the past, the government's influence was restricted to only the national boundary. Yet, in a more inter-dependent international business environment, the government's incentive systems such as the provision of transportation infrastructure and educational opportunity, attract MNCs to invest in certain regions and shape the global strategy of firms. This is why the institutional view of the firm has gained attention in the developed countries, although scholars have perceived the role of the government and socioinstitutions were more significant in the underdeveloped markets (see Chapter 2). In recent years, alliance capitalism takes various forms in inter-governmental relationships. They range from free-trade intergovernmental relationships (such as the World Trade Organizations) to regional and mega-regional relationships.

3.2.3. *Eclectic Perspective of the OLI Paradigm*

Throughout the years, Dunning revised and developed his theory which became more comprehensive. The OLI paradigm can integrate many related theories in economics and business fields. The ownership advantages align with studies of product cycle theory, industrial organizational theories, market imperfection theory, and follow-the-leader theory as well as static and dynamic views of firm resources (resource-based view, evolutionary theory, and organizational theories). Location advantages on the other hand comprise studies of traditional location as well as the process of agglomeration, complementary assets, government and oligopolistic behavior, and risk diversification. Lastly, internalization theory covers and expands such studies as agency theory, market power theory, and knowledge sharing and acquiring theories.

3.3. Motivations of FDI[8]

While reiterating that there is no single theory that can satisfactorily encompass and explain why firms go global, Dunning (2000) specified four particular types of foreign value-added activities that capture the main motivations of FDI. The first three are asset-exploiting in nature, generating economic rent through the use of the firm's existing assets, whereas the last is asset-augmenting activity, adding new capabilites to its existing assets.

The first is *market-seeking FDI*, which was designed to utilize a particular foreign market, or set of foreign markets. For example, firms would seek rapidly growing economies in developing countries to expand their market position. The earlier they enter, the more they would benefit from their prevalence in the market and establish monopolistic position. This is referred to as the first-mover advantage (Lieberman and Montgomery, 1988; 1998).

Second, *resource-seeking FDI* was designed to gain access to natural resources (e.g., minerals and agricultural products) and low-skilled labor. In recent years, however, there has been a decrease in the rate of expansion of natural resource sectors as many products have become less resource-intensive and there are many substitutes, such as synthetic materials and new alloys. Improvement in recycling techniques and miniaturization of components have also contributed to less investment in natural resources. The advancement of technology and the automated system of productions also substituted the work of unskilled labor force.

---

[8]This part is a summary of and an extension to Dunning's (2000) paper.

Third, *rationalized or efficiency-seeking FDI* was designed to promote a more efficient division of labor or specialization of an existing portfolio of foreign and domestic assets to decrease inefficiencies. Efficiency-seeking FDI has increased due to the reduction of both transport costs and artificial barriers. This term is relatively vague, yet Narula and Dunning (2000) explain that in the past efficiency-seeking FDI was done, particularly in developing countries, to seek human resources for manufacturing of export business. In more recent years, it has changed to "exploiting economies of cross-border specialization and the uneven distribution of immobile created assets" (Narula and Dunning, 2000: 152). Some scholars have criticized that efficiency-seeking motivation cannot be seperated from resource-seeking motivation and that it is only about gaining from cheap labor costs in less developed countries (e.g., Franco, Rentocchini, and Marzetti, 2008). Therefore, other scholars have put more emphasis on dispersed activities to exploit economies of scale and scope (e.g., Bevan and Estrin, 2000; Franco, Rentocchini, and Marzetti, 2008).

Fourth, *strategic asset-seeking FDI* is to protect or augment the existing O specific advantage of the investing firms. In order to augment resources to their O advantages, firms learn and complement their competencies from the host country, mainly in the developed countries. Because strategic assets refer to the advanced input factors, such as technology, high skilled workers as well as knowledge-intensive firm networks, this case was considered as an exceptional case in early FDI studies and to Dunning (See for more detail Moon and Roehl, 2001). Thus, strategic asset-seeking was categorized as an exceptional motivation which puts emphasis on "strategic" purposes. Rather than exploiting resources, firms invest to complement their resources for the purpose of reducing competition and outperforming their rivals through merging with other firms or allying with them.

Dunning (2000) arranged these four motivations based on the development level of host country. For example, if we were to divide host countries to three groups: Underdeveloped, newly emerging economies and the developed economies; the underdeveloped nations are likely to attract resource-seeking FDI, rapidly developing countries attract market-seeking and efficiency-seeking FDIs, and the developed countries attract strategic asset-seeking along with market and efficiency-seeking FDIs (Narula and Dunning, 2000). Thus, as the host country's economy and industrial structure become more developed, L advantage changes from the inherited resources to created assets.

3.4. Conclusion

Dunning's tripods of the OLI paradigm explains why, where, and how MNCs invest abroad. He made subsequent changes to the OLI paradigm, but maintained the foundational assumptions of prioritizing O advantage over L and I advantages, so the primary motivation of FDI is to exploit O advantages abroad. Yet, as the OLI paradigm incorporated the business perspective on creating knowledge-intensive assets from merely overcoming market failures, the theory further added dynamic and asset-augmentation aspects. Thus, FDI motivations have been elaborated from resource-seeking, market-seeking, efficiency-seeking to include strategic asset-seeking. The scope of analysis has also been expanded; from one MNC's investment in a host country to firm alliances that can be influenced by host country's government and institutional structures. Although OLI paradigm has been criticized for being not mutually exclusive and being too eclectic, it has contributed largely to establishing the foundational backbone of FDI studies.

Chapter 4

The Global Perspective on FDI: From OLI Paradigm to Imbalance Theory[1]

Summary

We have examined Dunning's (Ownership-Location-Internalization) OLI paradigm, the backbone of foreign direct investment (FDI) theory that was developed based on the investment from firms of developed countries that have proprietary assets over local competitors in host countries. However, from the 1980s, "new" MNCs from developing countries that do not have specific advantages over the leading companies in the global business sphere evolved and rapidly reduced their competitiveness gap with the MNCs from developed countries. Their accelerated pace of internationalization was geared by their critical disadvantages rather than their advantages over others. They were able to succeed by complementing their disadvantages rather than by exploiting their advantages. Thus, in order to examine the rise of new MNCs, we employ the imbalance theory, developed by Moon and Roehl (2001) which explains the determinants of internationalization path from both developing and developed firms' perspectives. This also shows that latecomers' advantages do not lie in the conventional perspective of ownership advantages but in the new perspective of firm advantages, which are the abilities to balance out the imbalances of firms' asset portfolio through attaining complementary advantages.

---

[1] This chapter is reprinted with slight modifications from Moon and Yim (2014).

4.1. The Imbalance Theory

The studies on FDI have burgeoned based on different types of inverstment paths. As countries become more industrialized or developed, their firms also built up competencies. This is why MNCs from developed countries have more advanced assets than those from developing countries.

In this respect, earlier studies of FDI were based on the MNCs from developed countries that have advantages over firms in host countries, mostly in developing countries. MNCs generated rents from exploiting their advantages and building monopolistic status in foreign countries. Yet, FDI flows from the 1970s started to diverge. While, the conventional internalization path was based on downward investment — from developed to developing countries, investments taking the upward path — from developing to developed nations (e.g., Amsden, 2001). Despite increase in MNCs' investments from developing countries, they were regarded as a byproduct of globalization at best, and exceptional or illegitimate at worst, as many of them were subsidized by the home government or were attracted to the preferential treatment in some host countries (Moon, 2004b).

MNCs from developing countries have different features from those of developed firms. They do not have critical "superior" ownership advantages that can outweigh the liability of foreignness. Then, what is the motivation for these developing firms to invest abroad? Moon and Roehl (2001) explained that as opposed to conventional perspectives on rent yielding FDI, the motivation of outward FDI from developing countries is not only to exploit the existing resources but also to complement what firms lack in the current status. They then introduced the "imbalance theory" in which its theoretical thread is found in Penrose's (1959) idea on the imbalance in firm resource portfolio.

Although Penrose (1959) herself did not pay much attention to FDI, her insights have laid profound foundations as to why firms invest abroad; to address imbalances. Moon and Roehl (2001) insisted that any affluence or deficiency of resources will motivate firms to go abroad in order to maintain the "balance" between the optimal level of output versus input. Firms with ownership advantages will go abroad to exploit their resources and firms with critical disadvantages will venture abroad to complement

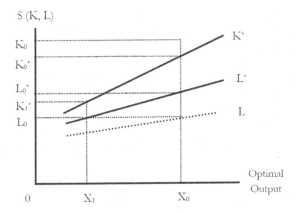

Figure 4.1.   Constraint Function for *ex ante* Optimal Output
Source: Moon (2004c).

their shortage in resources. The resources are used in a broad sense, such as technology, brands, distribution networks and market position that are critical for business operations.

Let us see how this can be explained a graph. Suppose a firm's optimal output[2] is at X_0 in Figure 4.1. Given a certain level of output, the optimal level of inputs (capital and labor) is determined. Here, there are only two factors, capital (K) and labor (L) in the model. If a firm wants to operate at X_0, the optimal requirement of factors at that level of output is K_0^* and L_0^*. In reality, if a firm has capital that is K_0, which is larger than K_0^* and has a labor of L_0, which is smaller than L_0^*, the firm produces output at the level of X_1 despite its abundance of capital that is the amount of "$K_0–K_0^*$." In other words, it is the deficiency of labor that constrains the optimal level of output for the capital abundant firm. The marginal productivity due to the surplus amount of capital, which is not utilized in this case, is going to be almost zero. If a firm were to invest its surplus amount of capital abroad or use it in the business that needs it, the firm is likely to increase its productivity and the optimal level of output. If not, the optimal output will be X_1 and the constraints is the function of L (dotted line). The firm will then have a surplus $K(K_0–K_1^*)$ which is greater than the original surplus $K(K_0–K_0^*)$.

---

[2] The "optimal output" is defined as the output associated with the lowest average cost.

Thus, if there are any discrepancies in the equation of the optimization, a firm will act to complement or allocate its resources accordingly. Taking an example of the two MNCs from Korea, Samsung Electronics Co. Ltd. (SEC) and LG Electronics (LGE), SEC had a larger market share than LGE in the domestic market by having competitive assets in semiconductor business. If we were to analyze this case from the conventional perspective of FDI, because SEC had a relatively stronger position at home, it is more likely to invest abroad than LGE. However, Moon and Roehl (2001) found that LGE invested more than SEC in Silicon Valley. According to their survey and analysis, LGE was more active in foreign investment in order to compensate for its disadvantageous position at home and not to lose its technological and market position against SEC.

Some may argue that this phenomenon may be explained by the "location advantage" of the OLI paradigm. Firms invest in Silicon Valley to exploit technology-related location advantages. Yet, OLI paradigm assumes that the condition of having a superior ownership advantage has to be met before looking for location advantages. Asset-augmentation-based FDI can also only explain up to the point why both firms invested in Silicon Valley, as it requires ownership advantages to augment new assets abroad. On the other hand, the imbalance theory explains "why" LGE invested more than SEC in Silicon Valley.

With regard to country-of-origin effects, the imbalance theory also illustrates why MNCs choose to go abroad beyond the motivations of asset, market, efficiency, or strategic asset seeking, presented by Dunning (1997; 1998; 2000). MNCs from less developed countries are perceived to be "inferior" regardless of their actual competencies as consumers reflect the image of a country on products (Bilkey and Nes, 1982). Whereas consumers, particularly in developed countries, are likely to show more favorable attitudes towards domestic rather than foreign products, studies have shown that there exists hierarchy of psychic effects among countries (e.g., Han and Terpstra, 1988). Particularly, products — made in, sourced from or branded by developing countries — will be less favored than the products from developed countries. The customers tend to evaluate them negatively, than their actual quality and associate them with their psychic distance.

General explanation of this behavior is that the consumers are less informed and less familiar with foreign products (Han and Terpstra, 1988).

In order to overcome the disadvantages of the home country, firms from developing countries increase their investments abroad in developed countries to establish a good brand name. This was the case of the Korean firms in the past, where they tried to demarcate their country's image from their firm image; some Korean firms did not emphasize their country-of-origin, but rather portrayed themselves as "countryless".

Firms' motivation of going abroad stretches far beyond exploitation of its own resources. Although Dunning (1993; 2000) himself has incorporated the concept of asset augmentation in his OLI paradigm, the imbalance theory takes a more proactive approach of exploring new foreign sources which are critically lacking in maximizing the output. In this respect, the imbalance theory is meaningful in several ways. First, it embraces the concept of dynamic perspective on a firm's resource exploitation and exploration process. Firms will go abroad when they have significant ownership advantages. Firms will also venture abroad to complement their shortages in resources. Any imbalances created in firms' growth will thus motivate firms to invest abroad.

In this respect, the imbalance theory also gives insights to why firms need to upgrade and complement their assets. Once firms take a monopolistic position, they tend to fall into competency traps (Leonard-Barton, 1992) or success syndrome (Tushman and O'Reilly, 1996) as they tend to focus on what they have been good at. On the other hand, when firms fail, they tend to change their businesses or investments without giving enough concentration of resources and efforts to make them work.

Yet, any competitive resources can lose value at any time. Firms' growth is a matter of how it can exploit its competitive assets but at the same time complement what they are critically lacking in order to respond to environmental changes. This aligns with the logic set out by March (1991) in finding balances between exploitation and exploration.

Exploitation is about increasing efficiency, control and certainty through refining firms' resources. Exploration is about innovation, autonomy, and embracing variations through searching and discovering new resources and knowledge. March (1991) explained that it is important to maintain a balance between the two in order to stimulate the learning capability of the organization. Many subsequent studies have been conducted in searching for ambidexterity of the firm, being capable of doing both things at the same time, or in time series (e.g., Raisch et al., 2009; He and Wong, 2004; Andriopoulos and Lewis, 2009). The balancing activity not only promotes firms to proactively shape business activities but also provides sources to constantly build new competencies of the firm through stimulating learning and innovation capabilities of the firm (see Chapter 2).

Moreover, the imbalance theory is useful in explaining why some firms show similar FDI strategies. A similar explanation from prior studies is based on the oligopolistic reaction to competitors' investments (e.g., Knickerbocker, 1973). As they compete against their rivals, they have to invest in similar resources abroad or preoccupy before others. So if one competitor invests in another country, the other is likely to do the same. Yet, this explanation is based on the leading firms or firms from developed nations and it does not compare why the late-movers or the followers in the industry can take similar paths with the (leading) firms that have different advantages. The imbalance theory, focusing on the imbalance between advantages and disadvantages of the firm, explains that followers in the industry (not only necessarily from developing countries) take similar routes in FDI as the leaders do to emulate other leaders by acquiring similar resources in which they critically lack in the current status. During the 1990s, Korean firms showed similar geographical portfolio of FDI as the Japanese firms did in the past, so they were able to rapidly catch-up the Japanese firms in terms of market share and sales.

On the other hand, the imbalance theory can be applied similarly to the host country's strategy of attracting FDI. While, location advantages were only assessed from the investing firms' perspective, Yim (2013) explained why some countries need to attract MNCs despite the negative impacts coming from the MNCs' (see Chapter 5). As developing countries have some critical disadvantages in their locations, host governments need to bring in MNCs to solve these problems which have been barriers in enhancing their competitiveness. The MNCs are indeed the most effective drivers of the changing and upgrading industry structures.

The home country image as a less developed country will also drive a critical motivation for firms from developing countries to invest in developed countries. Other home disadvantages include unfavourable institutional environment and inefficient or missing market mechanisms (Ghemawat and Khanna, 1998; Cuervo-Cazurra and Genc, 2008). While conventional FDI studies do not explicitly incorporate home country disadvantages for FDI, the imbalance theory expands our view on FDI motivations and the role of disadvantages on firms and both home and host countries.

Although the imbalance theory was mainly developed based on the imbalances in the "portfolio" of firm resources and strategic assets, this perspective can be applied and extended to the "entire value chain" of firm operations (Yim, 2013). If there are imbalances in firm operations, throughout the time, and among the businesses/subsidiaries, they can critically hurt the entire operation of the firm. Some businesses evolve faster or slower than others. Particularly, technology-oriented firms that have been intensively investing in R&D face difficulties in producing new technologies, as the manufacturing subsidiaries are not well-informed or cannot catch-up to the recent technological development. They may need to train workers to produce the upgraded product, or invest largely in machines and facilities to produce them.

This was the case for an automaker, Hyundai Motor, in Korea. To overcome such obstacles, Hyundai Motor holds seminars and training across all subsidiaries annually to overcome imbalances in knowledge level and train the employees from the part suppliers and dealers together, as well as their own employees. Trust-building across businesses and subsidiaries helped the employees' exchange and knowledge transfer faster, skipping technical procedures to exchange data across departments. Thus, addressing any imbalances in value chain has helped the company engage in knowledge sharing more efficiently and effectively across regional subsidiaries in which their "routine" of knowledge sharing has become one of their competitive assets.

4.2. Blessings in Disguise

The core difference between the conventional perspective and the imbalance theory on FDI lies in the ownership advantage. The concept of ownership advantage comes from the theory of market failure. Hymer (1976 [1960]) described that because there are resources that are accessible to only a few firms, they become the source of monopolistic rent-seeking behavior of MNCs. Based on this concept of monopolistic assets, Dunning's OLI paradigm explains that firms need to possess ownership advantages that can overcome any cost of foreignness (Dunning, 1958; Dunning and Lundan, 2008a). After Dunning acknowledged the difference between structural market failure and transaction-cost market failure, he incorporated the monopolistic asset under the ownership advantage and extended it to internalization advantage.

Monopolistic assets help firms take the leading position (entry barriers), and in the market they are interpreted under the context of "superior resources" vis-à-vis rivals in which they are described as knowledge-intensive, technological or organizational resources. However, as opposed to the concept of superiority, the Penrosian approach focused on the balanced sequence of resource development, use, acquisition, and absorption (Rugman and Verbeke, 2002). This is why Moon and Roehl (2001) explained that firms from developing countries do not have substantial ownership advantages vis-à-vis their rivals in the developed countries. Rather, their capability lies in their balancing activity of any imbalances in asset portfolio, which is largely undervalued in the conventional perspective on proprietary assets.

As the UNCTAD global survey in 2006 reported in the World Investment Report, three-quarters of the competitive advantages of MNCs from developing countries are not ownership advantages (e.g., superior technology) from a conventional perspective, rather they arise from production process capabilities (35% of responses), networks and relationships (28%), or an effective organizational structure (13%). Thus, we can re-interpret the concept of ownership advantage and emphasize that the capabilities of the firms from developing countries should be regarded as "different" sets of ownership advantages that are valuable and have become more so in environments of high velocity. This can be easily seen from the evolutionary perspective of firm resources, including dynamic capability (e.g., Teece, Pisano and Shuen, 1997), absorptive capacity (e.g., Cohen and Levinthal, 1990), combinative capability (e.g., Kogut and Zander, 1992), and so on (see Chapter 2).

The following section illustrates capabilities of firms from developing countries which were evaluated in the existing literature as secondary or peripheral capabilities to gain competitive advantages. Recently, they have increasingly become crucial in strategic management and organizational studies in general. The global economy is no more as stable as it in the past, thus, a shift towards a dynamic perspective in finding sources of competitive advantages is not only confined to a few emerging firms but applies to MNCs in general. These capabilities also explain better, how latecomers in the industry can catch up and find favorable competitive positions in the market.

4.2.1. *Advantages of Latecomers*

Overcoming Capabilities

Cuervo-Cazurra and Genc (2008) found that MNCs from developing countries have better operating skills under "difficult" governance conditions of developing countries than those from developed countries, because they are more familiar with these situations back in their home country. Whereas, MNCs from developed countries are not familiar with those situations. Developing country MNCs build resilience to difficulties and they know how to work around anti-market barriers for doing businesses. For example, firms that come from a country with high corruption are likely to have the know-how in dealing with corruption in host countries than MNCs from developed markets that are less familiar with high market inefficiencies. The World Bank (2005) also reported that MNCs from developing countries have an edge in other developing countries as they are culturally similar or they are geographically closer to each other. Such familiarity reduces hidden and overhead costs in business operations.

Operational/Execution Capabilities

MNCs from emerging economies have taken different paths in firm evolution from those of developed economies. Because underdeveloped countries have high market imperfection, and less well-institutionalized infrasturcture, firms have diversified into multiple businesses to expropriate rents that are coming from underdeveloped industries. MNCs grew out of the ability to set up new business ventures across a variety of industries quickly and at a low cost (Guillen, 2000). Through such experiences, these firms have built competencies, effectively setting up subsidiaries abroad and repeatedly entering a variety of industries (Amsden and Hikino, 1994).

Thus, they share resources across subsidiaries and firms which can help them build the overall and diverse knowledge over various projects, operations and businesses. For example, because there were not many skilled managers in the early stage of economic development in Korea, the top management team members were circulated across various subsidiaries upon their start-up and built diverse networks within the firm. This was how conglomerates from developing countries were able to effectively diversify and establish new subsidiaries due to the project execution capabilities of the managers (Amsden and Hikino, 1994). Overall, we can see that the cost per unit of subsidiary incorporation reduces with an increase in experience. This has helped the firm have a portfolio of expertise for constant upgrade and expansion of the firm.

Networking Capabilities

A strong network-building of firms has become a competitive source for latecomers (Yiu, Lau, and Bruton, 2007). Because these MNCs are conglomerates that have diversified into various industries, they share important information and experience from peer members who have undertaken international expansion. They are also vertically integrated and form a strong relationship with international suppliers and clients. This helps the investing firms enhance the bargaining power of the entire business network over the host country government and establish market legitimacy in the local markets (Yiu, Law, and Bruton, 2007).

Moreover, they gain precious information from other institutions at home, which they have built close relationships with. Guillen and Garcia-Canal (2009) specified that they have better political capabilities as they evolved in close connections with the government and political institutions. This capability has helped firms understand better and deal with different situations in host countries than the Western firms that were not familiar with the host country environments.

These capabilities were understood to be unique to successful latecomers in the industry. Yet, as the environment has become more volatile, these capabilities have been reorganized and further emphasized by Moon (2014; forthcoming), as new sources of competitive advantage. He implied that they should be extended to include leading MNCs, because the competitive sources do not lie in "what" resources but in "how" firms upgrade and manage these resources in the long run.

4.2.2. A New Perspective on the Source of Competitive Advantage

Firm capabilities from developing countries lie in overcoming disadvantages of both internal and external factors and balancing out any disruptions in business activities through time. These features have become the drivers for firms' growth. While, incorporating firm capabilities set out by scholars in the previous section, this chapter expands on the competitive advantages of the latecomers set out by Moon (2014; forthcoming) with "different" ownership advantages of firms, when investing abroad. By paying attention to the competitive advantage of both the latecomers and first movers, Moon (2012b) introduced four variables which are agility, benchmarking, convergence and dedication.

Agility comes from speed competitiveness. Agility is required in and across every activity of the value chain. Each operation needs to be speedy and precise and each of them has to conform to finding a balance across its value chain activities to maintain efficiency. Maintaining a balance in speed among different activities is also crucial. If one value activity is slower than other activities, the entire outcome will not reach its full potential. Agility has particularly become important in fast changing environments as an independent source of competitiveness as firm productivity is not only constrained by the minimum level of input costs but also with opportunity costs coming from lead time.

Benchmarking capability has not been appropriately considered as a source of competitiveness. Porter (1996) explained that doing things differently from others to deliver a unique value is a strategy, whereas, enhancing operational effectiveness is not. However, Moon (2014; forthcoming) explained that when firms learn from each other, they can constantly develop and find sources of competitiveness. It is also because today's international business is so complicated and highly interdependent that rather than bringing disruptions to the industry, bringing compatible yet complementary assets to existing global standard provides sustainable advantages (Yim, 2013). Thus, with a high learning competitiveness from emulating the best practice, firms can continuously sustain their competitive advantages.

Convergence, as anothr emerging source of competitiveness, refers to mixing and creating synergistic effects. Whereas, scholars often show negative views on the diversification strategy of firms and explain that they are diversified into multiple and unrelated businesses, Moon (2014; forthcoming) reinterpreted that these firms build capabilities to converge diversified businesses into one unit which creates large synergistic effects. He argued that the benefits can in fact outweigh the costs coming from (unrelated) diversification as firms build diverse knowledge and experience that can be shared and utilized across units. They combine and reconfigure resources for different purposes so that businesses can become more resilient to different and volatile business contexts.

Lastly, the motivation of firms in developed countries are motivated by giving incentive systems and making workers aspire for a superior compensation. However, the motivation of firms from emerging economies, such as South Korea, was rather stimulated by establishing clear goal sets with an emphasis on the disadvantageous situation of the firm. For example, Hyundai Motor and SEC set artificial crisis to alert employees even after they gained a substantial success. This is to put an emphasis on addressing new challenges that may lie ahead of them and complementing any disadvantages vis-à-vis their (potential) rivals, instead of compensating for what they have done well in the past and promising incentives to the best performing employees. Thus, firms have created a clear goal-setting for business and promoted a higher dedication among workers to achieve such goals, which has become the fundamental drive for firms' growth and sustainability.

Overall, the capabilities that are illustrated as unique to the MNCs from emerging economies, particularly the successful Asian firms, have gained attention as the success factors in general. As the competitive landscape has been changing rapidly, the dynamic perspectives on firm capabilities have become crucial. In high velocity environments, learning capability (i.e., absorptive capacity) and synergy creation capability (i.e., combinative capability) were emphasized to adapt to changing environments within a limited time period. The motivations of workers and goal settings have been largely emphasized by organizational scholars to increase learning and operational capabilities (e.g., Taylor, 1967). Therefore, it is very important to note that Asian firms have created sustainable advantages without advanced technology and particularly innovative capability, but with different kinds of capabilities that have gained more attention in international business, in which we could extend the conventional perspective on ownership advantage from having superior or monopolistic assets to having firm capabilities of addressing imbalances in the operations to complement the disadvantage and strengthen the advantages.

4.3. Extended Motivations of FDI

With an extended view on FDI from asset exploitation to asset complementation on firm-specific assets, FDI motivations can also be further extended. Dunning's FDI motivations are categorized as market-seeking, resource-seeking, efficiency-seeking and strategic asset-seeking (see Chapter 3). However, Dunning's FDI motivations are mainly focused on gaining greater rents. By applying the concept of the diamond model (Porter, 1990; Moon, Rugman, and Verbeke, 1998), a more rigorous analysis on firm motivations can be drawn. It is because firm activities are not only concerned with resource building and market expansion, but also for strategic reasons to enhance their competitive position and to deal with risks and opportunities coming from related and supporting industries. The FDI motivation can thus be categorized in to four: factor-seeking, market-seeking, related-and-supporting-sector-seeking, and strategic-business-context-seeking.[3]

First, the (input) factor-seeking FDI refers to resources, both tangible and intangible, which are critical for firm operations and productions. These factors can be sub-categorized in to basic and advanced factors where basic factors are related to country-specific assets such as natural resources and unskilled workers, while advanced factors are firm-specific assets such as skilled managerial capabilities and technology. This was extended from Dunning's resource and strategic asset-seeking motivations. The resource seeking is renamed under the basic factor conditions, and strategic asset-seeking under the advanced factor conditions.

The factor seeking can be both for exploiting firm's superior resources and complementing its disadvantages in host countries. For example, at the turning point from analogue to digital technology, LGE purchased a 5% share of Zenith (a US firm) in 1991. The investment purpose was to acquire HDTV and multimedia technologies, the brand name, and access

---

[3]The application of the diamond model to analyze motivations of FDI was initially done by Moon (2007). Here, the categorization has been modified and the examples used under Moon's (2007) categorization have also been re-organized accordingly.

to the US market. LGE increased its stake to 57.7% in 1995 and acquired the company in 1999 (Moon, 2007).

Second, the market-seeking FDI refers to market expansion, according to the conventional FDI perspective. However, as Porter (1990) explained, understanding the most sophisticated market stimulates firms to innovate and find competitive sources. In order to learn sophisticated tastes of consumers in diverse areas, firms strategically invest in the most sophisticated market in the world. For example, Amore Pacific, a Korean cosmetic company, invested in France in order to learn the sophisticated taste of French consumers for cosmetic products.

Third, the related-and-supporting-sector-seeking FDI has become increasingly important. When firms invest abroad, interdependent firms follow in order to complement operations with each other in foreign locations. This type of motivation can be sub-categorized into two: the host country's related and supporting sectors, and partnered firms' related and supporting sectors. The former refers to choosing a certain location over others to take advantage of the support sectors in the host country. For example, a Korean firm, Choong-ang Plastic Engineering that manufactures polyester tarpaulin bag for cement products, established manufacturing facilities in Guangdong Province of China because of the advantage of the province's transportation and financial infrastructure.

On the other hand, the latter refers to firm's investment in order to support its related firms from home countries. For example, Woori Bank, a Korean commercial bank, invested abroad to make Korean firms in foreign locations have an easier access to financial support. Also, as Hyundai Motor expanded its operations abroad, a number of parts suppliers also followed the route. This type of follow-the-partner FDI strategy can also be found in other manufacturing and service industries.

The fourth motivation of FDI is the strategic-business-context-seeking FDI. This FDI motivation is missing in the conventional FDI theory but can be understood in the context of business competition, or strategic positioning purposes. For example, SEC and LGE tend to engage in similar activities in similar locations to keep each other in check or offset the advantage of its competitors from going abroad.

More recently, firms have been investing in strategic locations to portray a certain image of a firm's products or to secure a base in these strategic locations. Hyundai Motor incorporated a factory in the US not only to serve the US market more efficiently but also to build an image that Hyundai cars are manufactured in the US. The preferential treatment (e.g., tax reduction) has also motivated firms to choose a certain location over others. Alabama's tax incentive system was one of the strategic reasons for Hyundai Motor's FDI. Strategic purposes can also be related to political and social pressures at home. For example PulmuOne, a Korean food processing company, built its business in the US to avoid various regulations on the food processing industry, enforced by the Korean government. On the other hand, a Korean company, Namyang, established a factory in Guatemala to overcome quota restrictions imposed in the host country.

This categorization, while looking into external and internal, as well as direct and indirect factors, shows a more comprehensive and systematic analysis of FDI motivations. We can see that Dunning's definitions of resource-seeking and strategic-asset-seeking FDI are under the categorization of the (input) factor-seeking. Efficiency-seeking, which is examined in terms of labor cost reduction, can also be categorized under factor-seeking. Dunning's market-seeking FDI is similar to the category of market-seeking, but missing the aspect of learning market sophistication. Thus, we can see that Dunning's categorization is limited in scope and covers only two subsets of the four categories of this new framework. This categorization, extended and revised from Moon's (2007) analysis, incorporates a more comprehensive and various motivations of FDIs, from both asset exploitation and asset complementation perspectives.

4.4. Conclusion

We have examined different paths of FDI and presented an extended perspective on what motivates firms to invest abroad. Firms invest abroad to balance out any of their affluence or deficiency in the system. This is because firms are driven to invest not only for exploiting advantages but for complementing their critical disadvantages.

In this respect, FDI motivations can be extended and re-organized into four, which are: factor-seeking, market-seeking, related-and-supporting sector-seeking and business-context-seeking. This categorization shows an integrated picture of how firms act to complement or allocate their resources in the case of discrepancies in the entire value chain activities.

This perspective can also bridge the gap between the OLI paradigm and the imbalance theory by reinterpreting the ownership advantage. By linking the ownership advantage with the four success factors presented by Moon (2014; forthcoming), this chapter emphasized different types of firm advantages that may be crucial for MNCs from developing countries as well as the leading firms in a high-velocity global marketplace.

As Darwinism theory explains the rational selection and survival of the fittest, it is not the strongest nor the most intelligent (i.e. differentiated) resources that make the firms grow, but the ability to complement and adapt to the changing external environments. Thus, the logic of the imbalance theory of the firm, together with new sources of capabilities of how to redress imbalances to adapt to the environmental changes can explain the FDI motivations and sources of firm competitiveness better than the conventional theory on FDI.

Chapter 5

FDI Impacts on Country: From Negative to Positive Perspective[1]

Overview

Foreign direct investment (FDI) theories have evolved from examining the exploitation of firm-specific advantages to redressing imbalances in order to complement firms' disadvantages. Most of these theories focus on how to enhance firm's competitiveness by engaging in international activities. The next important research question is how FDI impacts host and home country. In fact, it was not until the mid-1990s that FDI was regarded as positive and beneficial. After the two world wars, the European economy was devastated and experienced an inflow of US firms taking up a large part of the European economy under the Marshall Plan. Being over-whelmed by the influx of the US firms' influence, FDI was deemed as detrimental to the national economy of the European countries. Similarly, after the mid-1990s, when the Japanese firms were penetrating the US market and outperforming the US firms, it was the US that expressed similar resentment against the inward FDI of Japanese MNCs. Recently, as globalization becomes an inevitable trend in business, there have been mixed perceptions about FDI, some being positive while negative views remained. For example, in emerging economies, FDI is even considered as a new form of colonization, whereas the governments from more developed countries view it as a form of mutual growth and are encouraging FDI-friendly policies to attract investments. There have been many studies regarding the impact of FDI on both host and home countries from

---

[1] This chapter was prepared by Yeon W. Lee in consultation with Professor Hwy-Chang Moon.

different perspectives. This chapter, while acknowledging possible negative impacts, shows how the positive impacts outweigh negative impacts on the economic development of host and home countries.

5.1. Government Perceptions on FDI

Before studying the economic impacts of FDI on countries, different views of governments — mainly radical protectionism, free market and pragmatic nationalism — on FDI should be first understood because these perceptions have shaped how government and society perceive FDI and implement FDI policies. One extreme of the political ideology toward FDI is a conservative, radical position which is hostile to all types of inward FDI. The opposite end is the free market view that takes the stance of non-interventionist principle of capitalist economics. Pragmatic nationalism is what most countries nowadays have sided with, where the governments embrace policies between radical protectionism and free market.

5.1.1. *Radical Protectionism*

The radical view has its roots in the Marxist political and economic theory that portrays MNCs as being the instrument of the imperialist expansion. According to this view, MNCs exploit the resources of host countries solely for the benefit of their home countries that are often dogmatic and imperialistic (Hill, 2013). MNCs are seen as extracting profits from host country, leaving no economic or social value to the host country.

On the effects of job creation and technology transfer in the host country, the radicals criticize that important core technologies are tightly controlled by the MNCs and this prevents any significant technology transfer. Also, decision-making and executive positions are mainly held by the nationals of the home-country, hampering the qualitative development of the host country jobs and knowledge. Since advanced technologies are restricted from being transferred to the host country industries and local employees merely take on the job of low-skill sectors from, the radical view scholars argued that FDI by the MNCs from advanced capitalist nations leave the less developed countries relatively backward and dependent on advanced nations for investment, jobs, and technology. Therefore, less developed countries that allow FDIs from more developed nations would not be able to develop, and this is why these scholars advocate the justification to prohibit inward FDI, particularly from more developed countries (Hood and Young, 1979). Although these arguments seem extreme, this view was highly influential in the world economy from 1945 to the 1980s until the collapse of communism between 1989 and 1991 (Hill, Wee, and Udayasankar, 2012).

Recently, protectionist view has been revived among more developed countries. For example, there are ongoing protectionist reactions against the MNCs from emerging countries such as China and India, especially when these are state-owned and seek to enter the US market through mergers and acquisitions. In the case of other developed countries (e.g., Canada, France, and Germany), national security concerns are extended to economic considerations and the protection of "national champions." In these countries, screening mechanisms have been strengthened, and China, Russia, and other emerging markets are following suit.

5.1.2. *Free Market View*

The free market view goes back to the classical economics and the international trade theories of Adam Smith and David Ricardo. This classical view on world economy with the has been expanded to incorporate the economics of FDI. According to the theory of comparative advantage, it is argued that international production should be distributed among countries that have relatively higher productivity. In other words, countries should focus on specializing in the industries that they can be most productive. MNCs play important roles within this framework since they are the actors that disperse the production of goods and services to the most efficient locations around the globe. Therefore, as the free market view presumes, the MNCs will search for locations where production can be made at the lowest cost, thereby decreasing the overall cost imposed on the final product.

In theory, this view has become more widely acknowledged as countries have encouraged the global trend toward the removal of restrictions on both inward and outward FDI. In practice, however, there is no government that has purely adopted the free market view on FDI, particularly for security reasons. Restrictions on areas that are closely intertwined with national security are common among the G7 countries. Industries such as air and maritime transportation, telephone operations, radio and television broadcasting, financial services, insurance, and nuclear energy fall under government supervision for inward FDI (Richardson, 2011). For example, foreigners are prohibited from purchasing more than 25% of any US airline or acquiring a controlling interest in a US television broadcast network (Hill, 2013).

5.1.3. *Pragmatic Nationalism*

The radical protectionism and free market view are the extreme ends of the government perception. In practice, the pragmatic nationalism in which governments implement both agendas to alleviate threats and enhance national economy through FDI is more common (Branstetter and Feenstra, 2002). Most countries have implemented policies that are between protectionism and free market view. Governments with this view see that when a foreign company makes profits, some benefits go back to the home country. In addition, if the foreign company eventually becomes more competitive than domestic firms, domestic industries may lose their market position and the national welfare could be hurt. However, this view also acknowledges that FDI benefits the host country by bringing in capital, skills, technology, and jobs. Due to these issues on FDI, countries pursue policies designed to maximize national benefits while minimizing costs. Therefore, FDI is welcomed only to the extent that the benefits are greater than the costs.

Japan offers a good example of pragmatic nationalism. Until the 1980s, Japanese government policy was restrictive towards inward FDI. This was due to the government perception that the direct entry of foreign (especially the US) firms with ample managerial resources into the Japanese markets could hamper the development of the Japanese industry and technology (Itoh and Kiyono, 1988). This belief led Japan to block the MNCs from investing in Japan. However, during the 1960s, IBM became one of the few firms to get the Japanese government to waive the restriction on FDI and establish a wholly-owned subsidiary in Japan. IBM was able to do this because it was the only major source of mainframe computer technology at the time when numerous Japanese companies needed that technology for data processing. The lack of comparable alternatives available to the Japanese enabled IBM to open the Japanese market. This shows that from the perspective of the Japanese government, the benefits of FDI in such case — the stimulus that IBM might impart to the Japanese economy — outweighed the perceived costs (Hill, 2013).

Another important aspect of pragmatic nationalism is the tendency to aggressively court FDI if it serves the national interests. For example, host country governments often offer great incentives or subsidies to foreign MNCs in the form of tax breaks or grants to attract FDI. The UK has been the most successful in attracting Japanese investment in the automobile industry. Nissan, Toyota, and Honda now have major assembly plants in the UK and these Japanese automakers use the UK as their base for serving the rest of Europe — with obvious employment and balance of payments benefits for the UK (Hill et al., 2012). There was a similar case for Hyundai Motor when the company entered the US through a greenfield investment in Montgomery, Alabama. Hyundai originally considered over 50 sites across the US before making the final decision on the Montgomery plant (Clapp, 2002). This brought fierce competition among the state governments which wanted to bring in Hyundai's investment. Ultimately, as shown in Table 5.1, on top of Alabama's less active union activities, Hyundai chose Alabama that promised to provide great incentives for the company (Yang, 2006).

Table 5.1. Hyundai Alabama Plant Incentive Package

Public Incentives (in USD)		Private Incentives (in USD)	
Site improvements	55 million	Electrical improvements	6 million
Transportation improvements	29 million	Natural gas improvements	4 million
Training incentives	61.8 million	Telecom improvements	200,000
Tax incentives	76.7 million	Rail improvements	8 million
Other	12.1 million	Total Incentive Package	252.8 million
Public Total	234.6 million	Incentive Per Job	126,400

Source: Alabama Development Office.

5.2. Home-Country Effects

FDI entails both positive and negative effects on home and host countries. Overall, the net outcome of these effects vary depending on the characteristics such as the level of development of the country, economic and industry structure, government policies on FDI, as well as the motivations of the MNCs (such as asset, market or efficiency seeking), types of investment, and entry modes (UNCTAD, 2006). In this section, the effects will be examined at the national level of home countries.

5.2.1. *Capital Transfer*

FDI can benefit the home country's balance of payments if the foreign subsidiary creates demands for home-country exports of capital equipment, intermediary goods, and complementary products. In addition, outward FDI would generate financial inflows such as investment income, royalties, fees, and service charges associated with the investment (UNCTAD, 1995). Although outward FDI projects result in net financial outflows in the balance of payments of the home country in the initial phase, this gradually changes to net inflows once the direct investment yields returns in the form of income and other payments (UNCTAD, 1999).

However, capital transfer may evoke negative impacts in two ways, particularly in the initial stage. First, the initial capital which is necessary to finance outward investments leaves the home country with less capital geared for domestic investments. For instance, there is a deficit in capital if the outward FDI is carried out to exploit the production costs in host countries that are lower than those of the home country. Second, the current account suffers if the FDI is the substitute for exports (Hill, 2013).

5.2.2. *Trade*

The issue that concerns the effect of FDI on home country's trade depends on whether production abroad complements or substitutes for the exports of the parent company or other firms in the home country. Traditionally, trade and FDI have been characterized as alternative strategies (Fontagné, 1999). Firms can either produce at home and export, or produce abroad and substitute for exports. Under such scenario, economies of scale and transportation costs are key elements in the decision process.

However, the empirical evidence has much proven that complementary effects are greater than substituting effects, through intra-firm trade. Also, the relationship between outward FDI and trade largely depends on the motivations of FDI. For example, if the MNCs invest abroad for natural resources, outward FDI could increase the imports of those resources while exports of the inputs required for extraction would increase. In the case of market-seeking FDI, the investment can be expected to boost exports of intermediary products and capital goods from the home country. If the motivation is to enhance efficiency or reduce costs outward FDI would be expected to increase exports of equipments and other intermediary goods as well as imports of the final goods (UNCTAD, 2006).

As vertical and horizontal production networks are linked together across borders, FDI leads to more trade in intermediary goods (inputs) and final products to the affiliate. This type of relationship would be beneficial to exports from the investing home country and it shows that FDI and trade are complementary rather than substitutes (Fontagné, 1999). In fact, intra-firm trade, which comprises one third of entire annual world trade, is the area that grows stronger with FDI.

In case of Korea, the intra-firm trade of outward investing MNCs was reported to create a trade surplus of USD 6.8 billion in 2003 alone (MCIE, 2003). Here, FDI proved to render positive effects on trade. In the empirical studies on Korea's industry exports, Ha (2003) concluded that intra-firm trade between the company at home and affiliates in host country propelled trade, preventing the shrink of domestic manufacturing industries. In this period, intra-firm trade accounted for 46% of the entire trade balance where the core technology components and materials were procured from home to the local affiliates in the host country (MCIE, 2003).

However, exports from home country can fall with FDI since firms exploit their firm-specific advantages by producing in other countries. According to Lipsey (1995), for example, between 1966 and 1987, the share of world exports by the US in finished goods fell by 6% to 11%. In the same period, the global export share of MNCs from the US — the parent companies and their overseas affiliates combined — was quite stable. The fact that the exports of MNCs from the US remained unchanged while the exports of the US declined shows the impact of FDI on domestic exports. This was possible because although the overall share of world exports by the parent firms fell, the share of the local sales by the overseas affiliates and the exports from their host countries increased. This implies that the MNCs from the US actually had steady shares in world sales, while the US as a country was experiencing decrease in exports (Lipsey, 1995). This type of divergence between the home country and home-country MNCs occurred in other countries as well. For example, the Japanese export shares fell after the currency revaluations in 1985, but the export shares by the Japanese overseas affiliates increased and approximately offset the decline in the country's export share.

5.2.3. *Employment and Wage*

One of the greatest concerns of the home country government on outward FDI is the issue of employment. Although recent studies have empirically evidenced the positive effects of FDI on home employment, there is a problem of job loss, if for instance, firms invest in foreign countries to exploit cheap labor by relocating manufacturing plants abroad. Empirical evidence demonstrates a small and marginally positive impact of outward FDI on aggregate home employment, although certain activities and some groups of employees could be seriously hurt (UNCTAD, 1995), which eventually calls for the redirection of labor market policies. Particularly in developed countries, there are cases where outward FDI increased the risk of home country employment loss and even reduced wage levels (Scheve and Slaughter, 2004). For example, the textile and apparel jobs have been in steady decline for three decades between 1973 and 2005, reducing the US workforce from 2.4 million to 650,000 (USDA, 2012).

With regard to employment effects, the most serious concern arises when FDI is seen as a substitute for domestic production. For example, one objection frequently raised by US labor leaders against the free trade pact between the US, Mexico, and Canada is that the US will lose many jobs as US firms invest in Mexico to take advantage of cheap labor and then export back to the US (Baker, 1991).

Nevertheless, the popular view on the employment effect of FDI is that there is a positive correlation. Similar to the impacts on balance of

Table 5.2. FDI Effect on Home Country: Samsung's Outward FDI in Mobile Phone Industry

	2002	2012	Growth Rate
Domestic revenue (in trillion Korean won)	3.4	10.9	220%
Direct employment	6,000	20,500	240%
High value-added jobs (R&D, Tech, Design)	1,800	14,300	700%
Manufacturing jobs	3,500	3,800	86%

Source: Moon (2013).

payments, positive employment effects arise when the foreign subsidiary creates demand for home-country exports. For example, Toyota's investment in auto assembly operations in Europe benefited both the capital flow and employment in Japan because Toyota imported parts and components for its Europe-based auto assembly operations directly from Japan, thereby increasing the demand for workers in the related sectors at home.

FDI also has a positive impact on enhancing the quality of workers at home. An example would be SEC's outward FDI, in the mobile phone sector, since 2002. Within 10 years of direct investments for offshoring manufacturing jobs in other countries such as Vietnam, Korea was able to see the employment growth directly from SEC's outward FDI, most notably in the growth of high value-added jobs (Moon, 2012; Moon and Parc, 2014). Table 5.2 shows the accumulated growth of SEC's mobile phone sector from 2002 until 2012. Compared to the growth in domestic revenue and manufacturing jobs inside Korea, the rapid growth in the quality of jobs is portrayed. This is because when MNCs invest in developing countries, they create higher-value added jobs at home to manage and support these less skilled workers in host countries.

Although there are some empirical evidences that home and host country employments are substitutes (e.g., Harrison and McMillan, 2011), they also may remain as complements when the required skill sets of high and low skill are both simultaneously necessary and also reinforce each other. For example, the skill levels of manufacturing jobs at SEC's factories are different — manufacturing facilities in Korea require high-level skilled workers producing sophisticated parts and components and engaging in R&Ds, whereas factories in Vietnam focus only on final assembly which requires relatively low sets of skills (Moon and Parc, 2014). In short, whether outward FDI reduces or increases employment of the home country depends on the type of investment, the complementarity or substitutability of the activity and skill sets abroad in comparison with the home country, and the degree to which inputs are sourced from the home country (Dunning and Lundan, 2008a).

5.2.4. *Industry and Cluster*

The interaction of outward investment by MNCs with other firms at home serves as an important economic impact of FDI in all sectors of the economy. For example, the more suppliers and affiliates the parent company has in the value chain, it is more likely that the home country will experience greater impact. In Hong Kong, for instance, the growth of outward FDI in more advanced-technology industries — mainly the "soft" technology — has produced important forward and backward linkages with home-based firms (Chen and Lin, 2005). Gradually, these developments led to the emergence of clusters of production-related services (supply chain management, customer relationship management, transportation and storage, product design, and promotion), especially with the support of enterprises based in Hong Kong and operating in China (UNCTAD, 2006).

On the other hand, there is a critical problem with domestic industries that experience substantial outward FDI. The so-called hollowing out of the domestic infrastructure which eventually leads to a loss of related industry base may offset the clustering effect. As hollowing out often connotes the loss of manufacturing capabilities, it has been argued that part of this concern may only be interpretive (UNCTAD, 2006). In the case of Hong Kong, for instance, a massive transfer of labor-intensive manufacturing operations, mainly to China, since the 1980s has changed the nature of the home industry by weakening the manufacturing base (Chen and Lin, 2005). However, as the physical and human resources successfully shifted to service sectors, Hong Kong was able to transform traditional industries to higher value-added ones.

5.2.5. *Reverse Technology and Knowledge Transfer*

Home country benefits arise when the home-country MNCs learn valuable skills from their operations in foreign countries and transfer them to their home country. This is the reverse resource-transfer effect. Reverse transfer of technology (Hobday, 1995), where knowledge acquired by foreign affiliates is channeled back to the home country, is one of the most important ways of mitigating the risks of the potential erosion on the home country's technological edge. Furthermore, with the globalization of knowledge, technology flows have become a two-way phenomenon, where inflows and outflows mutually reinforce each other by bringing technological spillover effects to home.

Through their presence in foreign countries, MNCs can learn superior management techniques as well as product and process technologies. These resources can then be transferred back to the home country, contributing to the home country's economic growth (Bartlett and Ghoshal, 1989). For example, one reason General Motors (GM) and Ford invested in Japanese automobile companies (GM owns part of Isuzu and Ford owns part of Mazda) was to acquire process capabilities and production technologies. GM and Ford successfully transferred these know-hows back to their US operations, resulting in a net gain for the firms and US economy (Hill et al., 2012). In the area of managerial expertise and knowledge, outward FDI has been found to be an important channel. The Chinese MNCs acquiring skills from abroad are good examples where developing countries obtain managerial know-hows through multinational operations in advanced countries (Young, Huang and McDermott, 1996). Outward FDI can also have a positive impact on managerial practices and the skills of workers in the home country (Blomström and Kokko, 1997; Lipsey, 2002).

5.3. Host-Country Effects

Similar to the home-country effects, there are many benefits that FDI brings to the host country. However, host governments should not ignore the potential threats or risks that FDI may accompany loss of economic independence and short-term disadvantages.

5.3.1. *Capital Transfer*

Capital is a scarce resource in most developing countries. Therefore, acquiring capital by attracting FDI will directly help the economic development of host countries (Lipsey, 2004; Li and Liu, 2005). With regard to capital,

MNCs, by virtue of their large size and financial strength, have access to financial resources which are not available to host-country firms. Therefore, host countries can gain diverse channels for capital with the help of MNCs, in addition to the capital transfer from direct investment by the MNCs.

However, the capital inflow through FDI, in short term, is anticipated with the following outflow of earnings from the foreign subsidiary to its parent company at home. In order to avoid this type of outflow, some governments have responded by limiting the amount of earnings that can be repatriated to a foreign subsidiary's home country. This restriction may look good to the host country, but the host governments should be extremely careful and prudent. If the restriction is too high, MNCs will not invest in those countries. There are many alternative investment locations for MNCs, so the role of host governments is to gear more efforts on enhancing, rather than deteriorating the business environment.

5.3.2. *Trade*

The second potential benefit arises when the MNCs export goods and services to other countries. According to the UNCTAD report, inward FDI by foreign MNCs has been a major driver of export-oriented economic growth in a number of developing and developed nations over the last decade (UNCTAD, 2002). For example, in China, much of the dramatic export growth was due to the presence of foreign MNCs that invested heavily in China during the 1990s. In the mobile phones sector, for example, the Chinese subsidiaries of foreign MNCs — primarily Nokia, Motorola, Ericsson, and Siemens — accounted for 95% of China's exports (Hill et al., 2012). However, a concern arises when a foreign subsidiary imports a substantial amount of its inputs from abroad for the production in the host country. This will result in a negative effect on the current account of the host country. One criticism voiced against Japanese-owned auto assembly operations in the US was when the Japanese firms imported many parts and components from their home country, Japan. In response to this criticism, the Japanese auto companies changed their strategy by pledging to purchase 75% of their parts and components from US-based manufacturers (but not necessarily US-owned manufacturers). When the

Japanese auto company Nissan invested in the UK in 1986, Nissan responded to these concerns around local content by pledging to increase the proportion of local supplies to 60% and subsequently raise the proportion to more than 80%. In 2012, as a result, 83.6% of components were supplied from UK alone (Verdict, 2012).

5.3.3. *Employment and Wage*

FDI brings jobs to the host country both directly and indirectly. Direct effects arise when a foreign MNC employs host-country nationals. Indirect effects arise when jobs are created in local suppliers as a result of the investment and when jobs are created because of increased local spending by employees of the MNC. The indirect employment effects are often as large as, if not larger than, the direct effects. For example, when Toyota decided to open a new auto plant in France in 1997, estimates suggested that the plant would create 2,000 direct jobs and perhaps another 2,000 jobs in support industries (Jack, 1997). In 2005, when Hyundai Motor began its production in the Alabama plant in the US, 3,000 jobs were newly created in addition to the 5,500 jobs directly created from Hyundai's investment (HMMA, 2014).

When FDI takes the form of an acquisition of an established enterprise in the host economy as opposed to a greenfield investment, the immediate effect may be a decrease in employment because the MNC tries to restructure the operations of the acquired unit to improve its operating efficiency. However, even in such case, studies suggest that once the initial period of restructuring is over, the local firms acquired by MNCs tend to increase their employment at a faster rate than domestic rivals (Hill, 2013). For example, a study conducted by the Organization for Economic Co-operation and Development (OECD) found that between 1989 and 1996 foreign firms created new jobs at a faster rate than their domestic counterparts. In the US, the workforce of foreign firms grew by 1.4% per year, compared with 0.8% per year for domestic firms. In the UK and France, the workforce of foreign firms grew at 1.7% per year, while employment by domestic firms fell by 2.7%.

The OECD study also found that foreign firms tended to pay higher wages than domestic firms. For example, wages paid by MNCs in Turkey were 124% above average and their workforce has risen by 11.5% a year compared with 0.6% in domestic ones, suggesting that the quality of employment was better (Economist, 2000). Likewise, in Indonesia, after a foreign takeover of domestically-owed plant, both blue-collar and white-collar wages rose by average 10% (Lipsey and Sjöholm, 2005).

5.3.4. *Industry and Competition*

One of the most significant contributions of inward FDI has been the emergence of new industries inside the country or a drastically changed composition of production. Lipsey (2000) described the large role of US affiliates in the electronics industry in East Asia, especially in the early development of the industry. The earliest data available shows that the US affiliates accounted for a significant portion of exports in some cases, with the share declining over time. In another example, the development of plywood manufacturing and export in Indonesia in the 1980s shows that Korea and Taiwan initiated the business before the Indonesian companies took over.

There are other types of industry creation brought by inward FDI. In the case of Korea, when foreign firms entered the service industry, there was a positive correlation with the growth in other industries, namely the manufacturing industries. According to Park (2009), between 1985 and 2003, 16 manufacturing companies became more productive and expanded in size with the inflow of foreign firms in the service sector such as transportation, communication, finance and other business areas that are important for intermediary products. Thus, FDI also brings the inter-industry spillover effects.

In general, while FDI in the form of greenfield investments increases competition, it is less clear that this is the case when FDI takes the form of acquisition of an established enterprise in the host country. Since an acquisition does not result in a net increase in the number of players in the market, the effect on competition may be neutral. When a foreign investor acquires two or more firms in the host country and subsequently merges them, the effect may reduce the level of competition in that market, create monopoly power of the foreign firm, reduce consumer choices and raise prices. For example, in India, Hindustan Lever Ltd., the Indian subsidiary of Unilever, acquired its main local rival, Tata Oil Mills, to assume a dominant position in bath soap (75%) and detergents (30%) markets. Hindustan Lever Ltd., also acquired several local companies in other industries, such as the ice cream makers — Dollops, Kwality, and Milkfood. By combining these companies, the share of Hindustan Lever Ltd. in the Indian ice cream market went from zero in 1992 to 74% in 1997 (UNCTAD, 2000), thereby reducing the intensity of rivalry and competition in the industry.

5.3.5. *Technology and Innovation*

The host country benefits from technology transfer by MNCs operating in the country. This can stimulate economic development and industrial upgrade. Also, foreign affiliates exhibit higher levels of productivity than local firms (Aitken and Harrison, 1999). In this sense, multinationals often transfer significant technology when they invest in a foreign country (Potterie and Lichtenberg, 2001). For example, a study of FDI in Sweden found that foreign firms increased both the labor and total factor productivity of Swedish firms that they acquired, suggesting that significant technology transfers had occurred as technology typically boosts productivity (Modén, 1998). In addition, a study of FDI by OECD found that MNCs invested significant amounts of capital in R&D in the countries in which they had invested, suggesting that not only were they transferring technology to those countries, but they may also have been upgrading existing technology or creating new ones in those countries (Economist, 2000).

Spillover effects from inward FDI are usually evaluated as the positive influence from the presence of MNCs on the productivity of local enterprises. According to Caves (1974), the positive effects of MNCs can be categorized in terms of allocative efficiency, technical efficiency, and technology transfer. Allocative efficiency gains arise from pro-competitive effects. Technical efficiency comes from the demonstration of superior practices by MNCs. Also, with technology transfer, the presence of MNCs furnishes local firms with access to advanced technology on favorable terms (Feinberg and Majumdar, 2001).

Inward FDI also affects host country's innovativeness, which is vital to the growth of economies (Grossman and Helpman, 1994; Salomon and Shaver, 2005). This is extremely important because innovativeness purports future competitiveness. Foreign Management skills acquired through FDI may also produce important benefits for the host country. Foreign managers trained in the latest management techniques can help improve the efficiency of operations in the host country. Beneficial spin-off effects may also arise when local personnel, who are trained to take managerial, financial, and technical posts in the subsidiary of a foreign MNC, leave the firm and establish indigenous firms. Similar benefits may arise if the superior management skills of a foreign MNC stimulate local suppliers, distributors, and competitors to improve their own management skills.

5.4. Conclusion

FDI, until the mid-1990s was not considered to have positive impacts on the host country. During this period, FDI was mostly conducted by MNCs from advanced countries. Where the world was still in the dispute between ideologies, FDI was seen as another form of capitalistic invasion and economic imperialism. Nonetheless, this radical view has changed by embracing the benefits and advantages brought from FDI to both host and home countries. Gradually, governments have started to align their policies to mutually invigorate investment activities of both domestic and foreign MNCs in the direction to benefit the economy.

In this chapter, the FDI impacts on both home and host countries have been examined. As addressed throughout this chapter, the effects vary depending on the scope, type, and phase of FDI. For example, FDI may induce capital loss in the home country, however, those losses, when managed effectively, are short-lived and can be offset by long-term profits accrued from the outward FDI. Similarly, employment may dwindle depending on the type of FDI. However, there are both substituting and complementary effects that government or interest holders should consider. The five impacts on home and host countries do not only show a comprehensive picture by demonstrating both positive and negative impacts, but they also give significant implications to the government.

Along with the five major impacts on home and host country, there are other variables for consideration. Environment pollution, for instance, is an important social cause which evokes serious problems when mismanaged. However, this can be handled to minimize its negative effects if governments set out appropriate policy measures. All in all, FDI can create synergies through working on other important socio-economic factors for the national economy.

What is important in learning these potential consequences of FDI is to analyze how to increase overall benefits and reduce potential risks or costs. In order to do so, the best strategy is to establish clusters where firms, both foreign and domestic, work together by competing and cooperating with each other. MNCs can increase synergies among themselves and exhibit spillovers on the related sectors most efficiently and effectively when clusters are created, which will be discussed in the next chapter.

Chapter 6

FDI and Cluster: From Local to Global Link[1]

Summary

In the previous chapter, we have examined both positive and negative impacts of foreign direct investment (FDI) on host and home countries. While acknowledging the potential negative impacts, national strategies should be geared towards maximizing the positive impacts of FDI to override negative impacts. In order to enhance positive impacts, we emphasize the importance of cooperation along with competition among firms. While FDI studies are limited to analyzing an individual firm or a country, we expand the view to incorporate firm alliances and networks which can be further expanded to networks between clusters of firms in international context. Thus, we start from analyzing the clusters of firms and how they can be expanded to linking clusters across national boundary. We enlarge the view on clusters and provide a stage model for cluster network developments which expands from regional to international, then to global linking clusters.

6.1. The Role of Location

As multinational corporations (MNCs) transfer and mobilize resources across national borders, the traditional role of location has been understated from the corporate view (Porter, 2000b). However, an attractive location not only enhances firm competitiveness but also serves as the

---

[1] This chapter was prepared by Jimmy Parc and Sylvain Rémy in consultation with Professor Hwy-Chang Moon.

platform to enhance national competitiveness, by attracting competitive global firms to the location.

Competitive advantage of firms can be enhanced by having heterogeneous sets of resources to increase the productivity of the firm and differentiated value. On a similar note, for the location to be attractive, it needs to have heterogeneous sets of location-specific resources that other locations do not have or cannot imitate readily. The heterogeneity or immobility, however, does not come from the state-of-the-art technologies or "superiority" of other resources; it comes from how the competitiveness-building mechanism works in the location, which could be largely influenced by the institutional, social, political, and cultural aspects. In the end, global managers will choose a favorable business environment which encompasses various aspects beyond production input sources such as labor force, technology, and infrastructure (Reich, 1990; 1991).

Then how can we build attractive resources that are sticky to certain locations? Porter (2000b) explained that any conventional type of location-specific resources such as land, low-skilled labor force, and infrastructure can be easily imitated and substituted by other nations. Therefore, these conventional resources do not make the location attractive, particularly in the long run over others. What cannot be easily imitated are the networks of firms and organizations that increase efficiency and promote active knowledge sharing and innovation among firms.

Porter (1998b) approached this mechanism from the perspective of geographic cluster to emphasize that competitive advantages reside in the locations where businesses operate. The cluster of firms brings synergistic effects that can outweigh negative impacts brought by MNCs. Clusters also do not only mitigate negative aspects but actually create advantages and generate advantageous externalities. This is why Porter (1990; 1998b; 2000b) consistently argued that the sustainable competitive advantage arises locally in a global economy, which may sound paradoxical.

Porter's concept of clusters thus gives significant implications for policy suggestions. Let's look into how FDI is related to clusters; how MNCs can benefit from clusters; and how policy makers can develop cluster formation to create sustainable and location-specific competitive assets that are heterogeneous to certain regions.

6.2. Existing Theories on Clusters

Marshall (1920 [1890]) introduced the concept of geographical cluster by identifying the concentration of localized industries. This became the heart of the theories which laid foundations for subsequent studies. Among many scholars who extended the concept of geographical cluster, Krugman (1979) linked trade and geography for the first time and introduced the concept of "economic geography". He explained that firms tend to locate themselves in larger markets to exploit economies of scale, and individuals tend to move to more populated regions, which would offer them higher welfare benefits coming from greater consumption diversity (Krugman, 1979; 1980). Krugman highlighted the relationship between economies of scale and transportation costs that can result in either concentration or decentralization of communities (Krugman, 1991b).

Building on Marshall and Krugman's works, Porter (1990; 1994; 1998b; 2000b) introduced the four determinants to enhance national competitiveness and highlighted the critical role of the cluster in the context of national competitiveness. The four determinants are factor conditions, demand conditions, related and supporting industries, and firm strategy, structure and rivalry (see Chapter 2). Clusters allow companies to operate more productively in sourcing inputs, accessing information, technology, and needed institutions, coordinating with related companies, and measuring and motivating improvement (Porter, 1998b). Porter's (1998b; 2000b) concept of cluster is more comprehensive in terms of explaining the effects of clusters, while existing literature focuses mainly on the knowledge and technology transfers in increasing the competitive advantages of firms and enhancing demand conditions for consumption diversity (Moon and Jung, 2010).

6.3. FDI and Cluster

Location is an essential parameter of FDI dynamics, but a lot of research about the location of FDI is confined to the country level, possibly moving down to the sub-regional level in the case of large countries. In either case, the focus of study is on politically-defined geographical boundary, even though FDI is economically driven. Such political units possess economically relevant but broader characteristics, including political regime and governance type, foreign trade regime, and business-regulatory legislation. Additionally, reliable official statistics are usually compiled and aggregated at the level of state or local government, making these data less directly related to the competitiveness of regional clusters.

The analytical scope of clusters should be at the level of the aggregates of firms. Porter stated that clusters are "a driving force in increasing export and are magnets for attracting foreign investment" (Porter, 2000b). Yet, the concept of clusters as a determinant of FDI had not been the object of much economic scholarship (Yehoue, 2005), at least until the mid-2000s. Furthermore, measurements of global FDI flows to clusters are difficult or impossible to obtain, probably for three main, interconnected reasons.

The first is that the definition of clusters is subject to a debate (Martin and Sunley, 2003), undermining their identification. Clusters are defined in wide geographical scales, ranging from street level (e.g., New York City's Garment District) to multinational and amorphous regions (e.g., the French–German–Swiss BioValley). The second reason is that clusters are naturally developed by aggregated firms, so that many or most have no formal governance. Third, the data on FDI in clusters are scarce and not systematically collected.

From the 1990s, studies of clusters in theory and practice have proliferated, and a notable improvement was made by Porter (1990; 1998). Then the parallel surge of MNC-driven globalization has drawn attention to cluster-driven FDI, at least it was seen through the prism of FDI. In a 2001 survey on clusters in Europe, MNCs were present in nearly all surveyed clusters and the number has increased over the previous decade (European Commission, 2002). This reflects MNCs' interests to tap into cluster resources and the growing popularity of clusters among foreign investors (Goetz and Niedzialkowskiego, 2008).

Clusters are traditionally thought to emerge from the agglomeration of local firms, potentially attracting FDI only at some later development stage. However, FDI can get heavily involved from the outset and play a key role in some clusters' development. The Sinos Valley shoe cluster, for example, contributed 80% of Brazil's shoe exports, thereby the country was ranked as the world's third shoe exporter in 1992. In part, this was because foreign traders, in particular the US retail chains, had set up branch offices there. Foreign firms did not only help with exports, they were also involved in design and quality control (Schmitz, 1995). Thanks to Mauritius' export processing zone (EPZ) policy, FDI inflows rose more than 10-folds between 1970 and 1997. A key factor was the dynamism of domestic entrepreneurs, which attracted FDI into clusters nearby (Yehoue, 2005).

Clusters should not be confused with regions (i.e., sub-country areas) as defined by geophysical, ethnic, political, or even economic boundaries. In addition to aforementioned political unit factors, many local factors can determine FDI attractiveness, such as natural resource endowments, market size, infrastructure, and others. Industrial clusters offer specific benefits that may attract FDI for their own sake, or in combination with other regional or national factors. Cluster economics include Marshall's (1920) classic economies of agglomeration, social capital (Camagni, 2002), and a mix of horizontal competition and vertical cooperation intensified by proximity (Porter, 1998b). Yet, we need to extend the concept and scope of clusters in order to better understand the real world practices.

6.4. Need for a New Cluster Development Model

Although Porter's theory on cluster is more comprehensive than that of other scholars, it is not free from criticism. There are two limitations in Porter's theory of cluster when applied to the real world: the theory is static on the current status of clusters (Motoyama, 2008) and the source of productivity is focused on geographical concentration as opposed to distant outsourcing. In other words, the scope of cluster is limited to the domestic, rather than the international context (Moon and Jung, 2010). In order to solve these limitations, there is a need for a more comprehensive and systematic framework as an extension to Porter's cluster.

6.4.1. *Static vs. Dynamic*

Traditional studies (Marshall, 1920; Weber, 1929; Loesch, 1954) that identified the benefits of geographical concentration were based on static efficiency such as the lowest input or the largest economies of scale (Motoyama, 2008). Porter (1994), however, insisted that it is not the inputs or scale of the firm, but the ability to innovate and upgrade the firm's skills and technologies that can create competitive advantage through clustering. He validated this perception through examples of successful industrial clusters located in advanced countries: jewelry cluster in Italy, cutlery clusters in Germany and Japan, pharmaceutical cluster in Switzerland, high-technology cluster in Silicon Valley, and the film industry in Hollywood in the US.

These examples of cluster demonstrate how the competitive advantage emerges through clusters but they do not show the phase of cluster development (Motoyama, 2008). In addition, Porter said clusters can be developed due to historical circumstances, unusual, sophisticated, or stringent local demand, prior existence of supplier industries, related industries, or even entire related clusters which can be another seed for a new cluster, one or two innovative companies, or chance event (Porter, 1998b). You might notice that all of these important factors for clusters, including the "chance event", are based on existing sources and cannot be easily found in countries at the initial stage of economic development.

Porter also explicitly explained that "new industries and new clusters emerge from established ones as economies develop" (Porter, 2000b: 26). This means that clusters are developed in relatively more developed economies. Moreover, Porter's terminology, innovation, mostly highlighted in explaining cluster theory, should be carefully understood. Porter clearly said that "innovation is the result of unusual effort" (Porter, 1990: 75). This means Porter's innovation is the result which can be achieved only at the developed stage. Therefore, Porter's cluster theory faces limitations in explaining the cases of relatively new clusters in newly industrializing and less-developed countries.

In order understand the dynamics of the cluster theory, cluster should be understood not just for innovation, but as a tool that enhances corporations' general performance. In this light, by participating in the cluster, firms can increase their ability to perform better in many aspects of business, and by locating well-developed clusters, a nation can stimulate economic development. Therefore, we need to provide a new concept of efficiency-oriented approach which is more comprehensive and dynamic than a mere innovation-oriented approach.

6.4.2. *Domestic vs. International*

Porter argued that what happens inside companies is important, but clusters reveal that the immediate business environment outside companies plays a vital role as well (Porter, 1998b). This perspective is consistent with other studies (Amin, 1994; Saxenian, 1994; Scott, 1998; Storper, 1997; Nachum, 2000). In businesses however, many products and services are designed, produced, and marketed through global supply chains that seek the best quality talent at a lower cost. One of the best examples is Apple's iPhone which is "designed by Apple in California, assembled in China". In the beginning of 2012, Apple recorded the best quarter in history for a technology company (CNNMoney, 2012). Obviously, this contradicts with Porter's conclusion on cluster, "although global sourcing mitigates disadvantages, it does not create advantages" (Porter, 2000b).

When understating the role of distant outsourcing, Porter's theory on cluster also causes theoretical problem in the field of FDI. MNCs have two types of different motivations for going global through FDI: one is to exploit their existing advantages and the other is to seek new advantages (Moon and Roehl, 2001; Moon, 2004b; 2004c). The latter type is an unconventional FDI, which is to overcome critically important ownership disadvantages of firms that cannot be obtained from home country. Indeed, by balancing out their asset portfolio through FDI, firms compensate for their own disadvantages.

Therefore, the iPhones manufactured in China show that in some conditions distant outsourcing is better than remaining in local clusters, such as Silicon Valley. In this regard, Porter's overemphasis on geographic configuration may be misleading and needs to be extended to a global scope. To sum up, Porter's cluster theory was designed in the domestic context (Moon and Jung, 2010). This is mainly because Porter's cluster is based on home-based approach. Although he mentioned clusters that spans across national borders and with neighboring countries such as southern Germany and German-speaking Switzerland, he his perspective of geographical proximity.

6.5. Four-Stage Model for Cluster Evolution[2]

In order to solve the above problems, static vs. dynamic and domestic vs. international, an extension to the scope of clustering was modeled through

---

[2]This part is summarized and reorganized from two sources: Moon and Jung (2008) and Moon et al. (2013).

Table 6.1.   Four-Stage Model of Clusters Evolution

	Domestic Cluster		International Cluster	
Stage	Stage 1: (Porter's concept) Regional Cluster	Stage 2: Regional-Linking Cluster	Stage 3: International-Linking Cluster	Stage 4: Global-Linking Cluster
Examples	Silicon Valley/ Cambridge/ Kista Science City	Hollywood + Disneyland + Las Vegas	Singapore + Indonesia + Malaysia/Hong Kong + PRD*	Silicon Valley + Bangalore

Note: *PRD means Pearl River Delta.
Source: Moon and Jung (2010).

internationalization by Moon and Jung (2010), including an introduction of evolutionary stages of clusters (see Table 6.1). This cluster development model has four different stages: regional cluster, regional-linking cluster, international-linking cluster, and global-linking cluster. For each stage, we can validate this development model with cases at both country and firm levels.

6.5.1. *Stage 1: Regional Cluster*

The first stage is the regional cluster. This is similar to the concept of Porter's cluster. For example, the clusters such as Silicon Valley, Cambridge, and Kista Science City are included in this stage.

Developed Country: Silicon Valley

Silicon Valley is a world famous cluster. First, there are high-quality educational institutions such as Stanford University and the University of California at Berkeley. Silicon Valley also has large and sophisticated consumer markets, including San Francisco and San Jose, which provides direct feedback on newly released products. Moreover, the US Department of Defense, an assured market for the most state-of-the-art technology, offers generous funding in this region.

Not to mention, its array of support services for new high-tech businesses, including venture capitalists and investors, lawyers, head-hunters, finance and accounting professionals, consultants, and a host of other specialists, has supported industrial growth. This means it has a business ecosystem that forms a favorable business environment. Moreover, the Valley is a hub of ideas for new products, services, markets, and business models. Furthermore, the region generates a high flow rate of ideas in information technology, globally without any discrimination between local and foreign companies. This promotes a high competition and induces knowledge sharing at the same time.

Developing Country: Samsung Electronics Co. (1969–1982)

The Korean government established an electronics cluster in Gumi in 1967 to boost electronics industry and "Electronics Industry Promotion Law" was initiated by President Park in 1969. However, instead of locating its business in this proposed industrial park, Samsung Electronics Co. (SEC) established its headquarters and manufacturing facilities in Suwon, a city close to Seoul, which could supply needed labor force and provide better transportation infrastructure (Suwonilbo, 2010).

In 1981, SEC produced more than 10 million (accumulated) black and white TV sets and became the number one company in the world in terms of the number of exported TV sets. As SEC consolidated its position, more firms concentrated in Suwon area and they formed an industrial cluster. Until 1981, the company had operated manufacturing facilities mainly in Suwon area in collaboration with many other suppliers and subcontractors in the region. Once SEC gained competitiveness in Korea, the company expanded its business portfolio from white goods to more sophisticated goods such as fax machine and semiconductors.

The formation of Suwon cluster by SEC cannot be well explained by Porter's theory. There were no sophisticated local demand, and no prior existence of supplier industries and related industries. More importantly, SEC was not an innovative company at this stage. In the beginning, SEC was only an original equipment manufacturer (OEM) contractor, producing parts and components for Japanese electronics corporations.

6.5.2. *Stage 2: Regional-Linking Clusters*

The second stage is the regional-linking cluster. Within a nation, a wider scope of synergy can be achieved by combining some related clusters.

A good example is the entertainment cluster in the Southwest region of the US, which consists of Hollywood, Disneyland, and Las Vegas. Usually this regional-linking cluster is to size up the economies of scale in similar and related industries.

Developed Country: Southwest Region of the US — Hollywood, Disneyland, and Las Vegas

A collection of well-functioning clusters can create added values. This is most apparent in a tourism cluster; the quality of a visitor's experience depends not only on the appeal of the primary attraction but also on the quality and efficiency of complementary businesses such as hotels, restaurants, shopping outlets, and transportation facilities (Porter, 1998b), furthermore with other tourism clusters which are located nearby. This means that operators in the tourism and travel industry can increase their collective markets and capacities by working together. It can benefit all parties involved by increasing opportunities and revenues. The Southwestern US is known for its fascinating accounts of the incredible natural landscapes, as well as some of the country's most popular artificial landmarks, such as Hollywood, Disneyland, and Las Vegas. They are located relatively close to one another, but their attractions are different.

Hollywood is famous as the entertainment capital of the world; Disneyland for its theme park with various animation characters; and Las Vegas for its casino, thematic hotels, themed restaurants, pubs and hotels, virtual reality arcades, megaplex cinemas, convention centers, and sports stadiums and arenas. Geographical proximity and unique characteristics of these clusters enforce the total competitiveness of the tourism of Southwestern region of the US.

Developing Country: Samsung Electronics Co. (1983–1997)

Based on its strong competitiveness in Suwon area, SEC expanded its operation and established affiliated companies in Gumi cluster which was initiated and supported earlier by the Korean government. During this period of fast growth, SEC started semiconductor business which was considered a very important strategic industry for the future. However, since SEC did not have adequate technologies in this field, the firm set up R&D centers and tried to cooperate with American and Japanese technology companies such as Micron Technology, Intel, and Sharp in Gumi[3] (Lee and Kwon, 2006). At this time, SEC developed and strengthened two important regional clusters for more efficient operations: Suwon area for semiconductors and home appliances, and Gumi area for telecommunication devices. The company then linked these two clusters in order to enhance synergies and performance of the firm.

6.5.3. *Stage 3: International-Linking Clusters*

The third stage is the international-linking cluster. With the combination of cross-border neighboring clusters, synergy effects can be further enhanced. Some examples of this international cluster are the "Growth Triangle" of Singapore (the core economy) with Malaysia and Indonesia (the peripheral economies) and Hong Kong's linkage with Pearl River Delta (PRD). "Front shop, back factory" is the main motivation for this cluster. The international-linking clusters, compared with the regional-linking clusters, are not only internationally linked, but also use different comparative advantages of participating economies that can be internationally interconnected.

Developed Country: The Growth Triangle[4]

The growth triangle, also named as the SIJORI triangle, includes Singapore, a well-developed economy, Johor state in Malaysia, and Riau province and West Sumatra in Indonesia. It has been widely discussed and evaluated in the 1990s as a model for cooperative economic development. These three

---

[3] During these times, in order to have a better access to high technology, SEC also formed joint ventures and acquired firms in the US. In addition SEC was also very active in cross-licensing agreements with foreign firms to obtain other advanced technologies. As a result, SEC became the third company in the world that developed the 64k DRAM following American and Japanese predecessors.

[4] This part is based on the Department of Foreign Affairs and Trade of Australian Government, available at http://www.dfat.gov.au/publications/pdf/gt_3.pdf.

economies are significantly different in terms of their stages of economic development and their comparative advantages. This makes them complementary and synergistic rather than competitive. Singapore's comparative advantage lies in its highly developed infrastructure in transportation, finance and telecommunications, and high-level managerial and professional expertise.

Johor's advantages of low-cost land and labor have been undermined with rapid economic development. Johor's competitive strengths are now its good infrastructure and its capacity to produce medium to high value-added manufactures. Riau still has abundant land and access to cheap and unskilled labor. The attractiveness and policy orientation in Riau province vary from island to island; Batam seeks to attract high value-added manufacturing, especially in the electronics sector; Bintan focuses on tourism and is developing a labor-intensive manufacturing base such as textiles; and other parts of the province are developing agricultural and oil-based industries.

Developing Country: Samsung Electronics Co. (1998–present)

In 1998, SEC first produced 256k DRAM. Based on its semiconductor technology, SEC expanded its business portfolio to telecommunication, IT, and media sectors. SEC also continued to expand its operations by setting up more manufacturing facilities, especially for mobile phone sets, in foreign countries such as Brazil, China, India, Vietnam, and recently in Slovakia, and formed international-linking clusters by connecting these clusters to Korea. Korea has strengths in technology and management skills, and foreign clusters have strengths in labor cost, market opportunities, and other activities in the value chain.

In the early 2000s, SEC established seven design centers in the world's major cities such as Milan, London, Los Angeles, San Francisco, Tokyo, Shanghai, and Seoul. The professional designers constantly monitored the latest design trends in their cities and reflected cultural and lifestyle changes to their products. At this stage, SEC successfully linked the competencies of these internationally competitive clusters to overcome the company's weaknesses.

6.5.4. *Stage 4: Global-Linking Cluster*

The final stage is the global-linking cluster. This is the connection of clusters around the globe to maximize cluster synergy and enhance performance of corporations regardless of their physical distance across the globe. A good example is the global connection between Silicon Valley (the US) and Bangalore (India) in the field of IT and IT-related businesses.

Developed Country: Silicon Valley and Bangalore

Firms engage in off-shoring and outsourcing in order to expand markets, pursue higher value-added activities, and access pools of human resources around the world. This trend has become prominent particularly in the IT industry, because the capacity for moving information between countries has significantly increased, due to the precipitously declined cost of bandwidth (Asia–Pacific Research Center, 2003).

Indeed, linkages between Silicon Valley and Bangalore have fueled the growth of software services both in California and India. Bangalore has risen in software services and call centers (D'Costa, 2004), whereas Silicon Valley has specialized in high-technology products. These advantages facilitate sustained foreign investments toward both clusters, and the productivity and efficiency have been improving (D'Costa, 2011).

Developing Country: Samsung Electronics Co.

SEC has networks all over the world. Among them, the most important networks are globally linked clusters. For example, SEC has manufacturing facilities in Galanta of Western Slovakia which is a famous electronics cluster. Other MNCs operating in this region include Foxconn (in Nitra), Sony (in Trnava), and AU Optronics (in Trenčín). In the beginning, these firms only sought labor but later they took advantage of this enlarged cluster. In this cluster, there are also secondary and vocational schools specialized in electrical engineering and quality universities which supply the needed personnel to the firms. SEC, then, links the advantage of this cluster to its parent company in Korea, located on the other side of the globe.

Suzhou in China has been transformed from technology receiver to high-tech generator, particularly for nanotechnology and related sectors

(Tekes, 2010). This cluster has been supported by well-developed universities and laboratories, such as Soochow University, Southeast University, and Advanced Laboratory for Environmental Research and Technology (Netherlands Enterprise Agency, 2011). Suzhou Innovation Park has incubated and supported over 100 nanotech-related companies from all over the world, including, 3M, SEC, Siemens, Johnson & Johnson, Phillips, AMD, Bosch, Eli Lily, and others.

In order to utilize this Suzhou cluster for its global operation, SEC established Samsung Semiconductor China R&D Co. (SSCR) in the Suzhou Innovation Park, which is also the place of China's largest LCD production (Samsung, 2011). SSCR focuses on semiconductor package technology, which complements SEC's other R&D centers around the world and local manufacturing lines in China (Samsung, 2003). Overall, SEC's Korean clusters in Gumi and Suwon take a role of "mother factory"[5] and "center of excellence",[6] in collaboration with these global-linking clusters for manufacturing and R&D.

6.6. Conclusion

The conventional theories of clusters were mainly based on local or geographically proximate firm networks. This chapter extended this view on clusters from local to international perspective. Here, the role of FDI is very important, because clusters can be more efficient when foreign firms work together with domestic firms, by competing and cooperating, and by sharing and learning knowledge with each other. This chapter also extended the traditional cluster model, embracing the importance of outsourcing, and by enlarging the scope from regional to global cluster linkages.

The new perspectives on clusters are important for the following reasons. First, by recognizing various sources of competitiveness, we embrace the formation of clusters not only in innovation-based developed economies but also in the developing economies. Second, by acknowledging the

---

[5] Mother factory: This facility develops new innovative production system and technology, and transfers them to other overseas facilities.

[6] Center of excellence: This center enhances the capability of individual domestic and international research facilities which have different core technologies and roles.

importance of distant outsourcing, we can better explain why exploiting and linking clusters are important. Lastly, by providing cluster stage model, government policy makers can determine how they can overcome their disadvantages, while enhancing their advantages at home by linking foreign clusters together through active interactions with MNCs and other organizations. Thus, the secret to cluster development strategy is not simply to develop new technologies, but to internalize others' strengths and combine these competencies to maximize cluster competitiveness. The linkage of firms and clusters is where the fundamental source of competitive advantages is embedded, and this cannot be readily imitated and substituted.

Chapter 7

Assessing the Investment Attractiveness: From Theory to Practice[1]

Summary

We have so far looked into the impacts of FDI and how positive impacts can be maximized through clustering of MNCs. Then how do global managers of MNCs assess their investment locations? In order to develop an improved and distinguished model compared to the preceding studies, this chapter first reviews the previous literature on assessing investment attractiveness. Then the methodology of selecting criteria and measurement is introduced for quantifying and rating countries' investment attractiveness. This chapter will then show how the framework and methodology can be applied to real business assessments. Finally, more general implications are derived to give guidelines for policy makers.

7.1. Review of Previous Studies on Assessing Investment Attractiveness

How do global managers choose the investment location? Managers say they target "attractive" locations. Then how can we measure attractiveness?

---

[1] This chapter was prepared by Wenyan Yin in consultation with Professor Hwy-Chang Moon. The contents are abstracted and extended from the earlier two projects led by Professor Hwy-Chang Moon: the project for advising Korean government (Ministry of Knowledge Economy) to enhance its investment attractiveness in 2009, and the project for advising Azerbaijan government to improve its business environment in 2012.

Table 7.1. Four Perspectives of Existing Studies

Perspectives	Existing Studies
Government regulation	— World Bank: Ease of Doing Business Index — Heritage Foundation: Index of Economic Freedom
Country risk	— Political Risk Service Group (PRSG): Political Risk Service (PRS) — PRSG: International Country Risk Guide (ICRG)
Economic attractiveness	— UNCTAD: Inward FDI Potential Index
National competitiveness	— IMD: World Competitiveness Yearbook (WCY) — WEF: Global Competitiveness Report (GCR) — IPS: National Competitiveness Research (NCR)

Firms need to exploit and augment their competitive assets through FDI. This means that multinational managers seek foreign locations where they can exploit their resources the best, and/or complement and augment new assets. From the country's perspective, the country needs to build competitive business environment to attract MNCs for economic growth of the region and country.

The previous studies on investment attractiveness assessment can be classified into four perspectives: government regulation, country risk, economic attractiveness, and national competitiveness (see Table 7.1). In the following, the framework and methodology of each perspective will be illustrated in more detail.

7.1.1. *Government Regulation*

There are two principal studies on government regulations. One is *The Ease of Doing Business Index* by World Bank and the other is *The Index of Economic Freedom* by The Wall Street Journal and The Heritage Foundation. The *Ease of Doing Business Index* emphasizes the regulatory environment for local firms and the *Index of Economic Freedom* comprises variables concerning regulations for both local and foreign firms.

The *Ease of Doing Business Index* measures the level of the regulatory environment favorable to the starting and operation of local firms. The *Ease of Doing Business Index* 2014 ranks 189 economies based on 10 indicators, which include starting a business, dealing with construction permits, getting electricity, registering property, getting credit, protecting investors, paying taxes, trading across borders, enforcing contracts, and resolving insolvency (see Table A.1). Each indicator represents different perspectives of business regulatory environment. The overall ranking is conducted based on a simple method; it offers equal weights to all the 10 indicators, and to the components within each indicator. The higher the ranking of the economies, the lower level of regulations and the stronger protection of property rights there are in the country. (World Bank, 2013).

The Index of Economic Freedom measures the level of a country's economic freedom, which is the fundamental right of an individual. The index is composed of four key aspects of the economic environment where the government implements its policy. The four aspects are: 1) rules of law, 2) government size, 3) regulatory efficiency, and 4) market openness, which are further divided into 10 components of economic freedom (see Table A.2). Each factor is scored from 0 to 100, and the overall index is the average of the scores of the 10 economic freedom variables. The country with a higher score has a higher level of economic freedom. This study also shows that more economic freedom is associated with higher income and better standards of life (The Wall Street Journal and The Heritage Foundation, 2013).

7.1.2. *Country Risk*

There are two studies on this approach, *Political Risk Services* (PRS) and *International Country Risk Guide* (ICRG), published by Political Risk Service Group (PRSG). The former focuses on industry-specific forecasts, and the latter on the current macro-level assessment.

PRS is a well-known approach for measuring and forecasting political risks. PRS provides political forecasts for three investment areas: financial transfers (banking and lending), FDI, and exports to the host country market. Specifically, it provides the current level and the changes of political risks that can influence the business environment over the two periods in the future which are 18 months and five years. The indicators for the forecast of the two periods are different. The 18-month forecast includes

12 factors, and the five-year forecast includes five factors (see Table A.3). Both forecasts grade the countries from the least risky (A+) to the most risky (D−) (Political Risk Service Group, 2014a).

ICRG provides political, economic, and financial risk ratings for international business. The rating system is composed of 22 variables which are further divided into three subcategories — political, financial, and economic (see Table A.4). The political risk rating assesses the political stability; economic risk rating assesses the country's current economic strengths and weaknesses; and the financial risk rating assesses the country's ability to finance its official, commercial, and trade debt obligations. The composite scores calculated from the three indices in the three sub-categories range from 1 to 100. The higher score represents the lower risk (Political Risk Service Group, 2014b).

7.1.3. *Economic Attractiveness*

FDI assessment from the economic attractiveness approach mainly captures the economic factors affecting the investment attractiveness of host countries. The most representative study this approach is the *Inward FDI Potential Index* by UNCTAD, which includes 12 economic variables. This Index is published in the annual World Investment Report by UNCTAD since 2002. This index is composed of four determinants, including market attractiveness, availability of low-cost labor and skills, presence of natural resources, and enabling infrastructure (see Table A.5). Each determinant is measured by at least three indicators. The composite score is calculated by combining the four determinants, with equal weights on each factor.

UNCTAD also publishes the *FDI Attraction Index*,[2] which ranks countries by the real FDI received in absolute and relative terms to their economy. Therefore, FDI Attraction Index is the revealed competitiveness in attracting FDI, while the Inward FDI Potential Index is the potential competitiveness in attracting FDI. By comparing the rankings of the two indices, a country

---

[2] It is the average of a country's rankings in total FDI inflows (absolute term) and in FDI inflows as a share of GDP (relative term). UNCTAD utilized the data of FDI flows of three years from 2009 to 2011 in World Investment Report 2012.

can conclude whether it receives more or less FDI compared to its potential attractiveness. The "above-expectation" economies are those countries which receive more FDI than their potential attractiveness. In contrast, the "below-expectation" economies are countries which have lower performance than their potential FDI attractiveness. For the countries under "in line with expectations", their performances in attracting FDI match their FDI potential attractiveness.

7.1.4. *National Competitiveness*

Compared to the previous studies, the national competitiveness approach is more comprehensive in that it encompasses economic, social, cultural, and institutional determinants affecting the FDI attractiveness. As shown in Table 7.1, there are three major studies on national competitiveness assessment: World Competitiveness Yearbook (WCY) by the International Institute for Management Development (IMD), Global Competitiveness Report (GCR) by the World Economic Forum (WEF), and National Competitiveness Research (NCR) by the Institute for Industrial Policy Studies (IPS). Although all the three studies assess the national competitiveness, their definitions and the measurements for national competitiveness are different (see Table A.6).

The WCY was the first study to quantify and rank nations' overall competitiveness. It defines national competitiveness as a country's ability to create and maintain an environment that facilitates the firm's value creation and people's prosperity. WCY 2013 evaluates around 60 economies, and most of them are advanced and newly industrializing economies. The competitiveness model is composed of four factors, which are Economic Performance, Government Efficiency, Business Efficiency, and Infrastructure. Each factor is broken down into five sub-factors, thereby 20 sub-factors, which are further measured by 333 quantitative and qualitative criteria (87 are for background information). The composite score of national competitiveness ranges from 0 to 100. The higher score means the higher national competitiveness (IMD, 2013).

The GCR was first published in 1996. According to GCR 2013–2014, national competitiveness is defined as the set of institutions, policies, and factors that determine the level of productivity of a country. The competitiveness model in GCR 2013–2014 is composed of 12 pillars and 114 criteria.

The 12 pillars are Institutions, Infrastructure, Macroeconomic Environment, Health and Primary Education, Higher Education and Training, Goods Market Efficiency, Labor Market Efficiency, Financial Market Development, Technological Readiness, Market Size, Business Sophistication, and Innovation. Compared to the WCY, the GCR includes more developing countries. In 2013 report, out of 148 countries in total, only 37 countries are considered as developed and the remaining as developing countries. The composite score ranges from 1 to 7; the higher the score, the higher the competitiveness (WEF, 2013).

The NCR was first published by the IPS in 2000. Compared to the previous two studies, the NCR has strong theoretical background and methodologies for assessing national competitiveness. The NCR defines the national competitiveness as a nation's relative competitive position in the international market among the nations with similar size and competitiveness. The analytical tool is the double diamond-based nine-factor model (or the IPS Model), which is based on Porter's diamond model and the extended models (i.e., Cho and Moon, 2013a; 2013b). The IPS Model is composed of eight factors — four physical and four human factors. These eight factors are measured by 116 criteria. The higher score presents the higher competitiveness.

7.2. A New Framework for Assessing Investment Attractiveness

7.2.1. *Framework*

The existing studies on government regulation, country risk, or economic perspectives emphasize some particular determinants for investment attractiveness. The studies on national competitiveness are also limited because some important variables are missing in explaining FDI attractiveness. For instance, the endowment of natural resources, which is an important factor for resource-seeking FDI, is not included in the IMD report. Labor cost, which is a crucial determinant for efficiency-seeking FDI, is excluded in the WEF report. IPS report does not include the variables about government incentives for attracting FDI.

In order to overcome limitations of these three models, we use the extended Porter's diamond model to examine specific FDI targets, and to

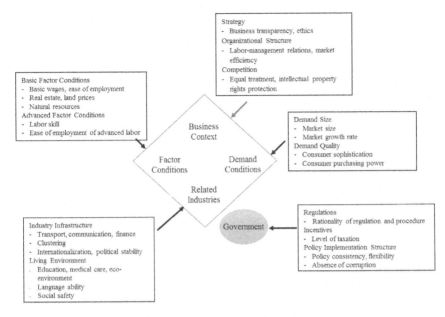

Figure 7.1   A New Model for Assessing Investment Attractiveness

find a strategic fitness between the firm's motivations and the location's relative competitive assets. Other than four controllable determinants, there are two exogenous variables in Porter's diamond model, which are the government and chance event. In our study, the government factor is added as a controllable variable for assessment whereas the chance factor remains as the exogenous factor. Thus, in our new model, five factors are controllable and positively related to enhance the investment attractiveness.[3] In order to define the competitiveness more explicitly, the five factors are further divided into two or three sub-factors. Each sub-factor highlights different aspects of competitiveness and altogether there are 12 sub-factors (see Figure 7.1).

Factor conditions are divided into basic and advanced factors. Demand conditions are specified into demand size and quality. Related industries refer to the presence of internationally competitive supplier industries, which are classified into both industry infrastructure and living environment.

---

[3] The five factors are modified from Porter's diamond model.

Business context refers to the nature of competition and conditions for business creation and management. It is further divided into firm strategy, organizational structure, and competition. Lastly, government refers to regulations, incentives, and policy implementation structure for promoting FDI. Regulations and incentives mainly capture the regulation and taxation, and policy implementation structure refers to the consistency and flexibility of government policy, and the degree of corruption of the government officers.

Table 7.2 compares the extended analytical model with the previous studies. The five studies (The Ease of Doing Business Index, The Index of Economic Freedom, PRS, ICRG, and Inward FDI Potential Index) overemphasize some factors while omitting other important variables to measure the investment attractiveness of countries. In this framework, factor conditions, demand conditions, and related industries are directly related to firm motivations of going abroad to exploit and acquire resources that are mentioned in FDI studies. On the other hand, business context and

Table 7.2. Comparison Between New Model and Previous Studies

Factor	Sub-factor	S1	S2	S3	S4	S5	S6	S7	S8
Factor Conditions	Basic					◐	◐	◐	●
	Advanced						●	●	●
Demand Conditions	Demand Size					◐	●	●	●
	Demand Quality				◐	◑	◑	◐	●
Related Industries	Industry Infrastructure					◐	●	◐	●
	Living Environment			◐	◐		●	◐	●
Business Context	Strategy						●	◐	●
	Organizational Structure						●	●	●
	Competition						●	●	●
Government	Regulations	●	●	●	●		●	●	●
	Incentives	◐	◐				●	●	
	Policy Implementation Structure	◐	◐		◐		●	◐	◐

Notes: 1) S1: World Bank, S2: The Wall Street Journal and The Heritage Foundation, S3: PRSG (Political Risk Service), S4: PRSG (ICRG), S5: UNCTAD, S6: IMD, S7: WEF, S8: IPS; 2) ●: mostly mentioned, ◐: partially mentioned, ◑: weakly mentioned, (blank) not mentioned.

government regulations influence firms' overall operational decisions to choose the most preferential location target. They altogether have to be considered in finding and building the most attractive location.

7.2.2. *Methodology*

Criteria

In order to measure these determinants for attractiveness, each sub-factor is further divided into a range of proxy variables. The criteria are chosen based on the definitions of each sub-factor. This framework includes 55 criteria. The hard data are collected from the statistics published by the well-recognized international organizations, such as the World Bank and the IMF. The survey data are selected from the relevant surveys conducted by the organizations such as the IMD, IPS, the World Bank, and Transparency International.

Factor conditions refer to the nation's position in factors of production necessary to compete in an industry. Porter (1990) classified it into basic and advanced factors. The basic factor conditions are measured by seven criteria and the advanced factor conditions are evaluated by four criteria as shown in Table 7.3.

Demand conditions represent the nature of market demand in a country for the industry's product or service, and are divided into demand size and quality (Porter, 1990). The demand size is assessed by six criteria and the demand quality is evaluated by five criteria (see Table 7.4).

According to Porter (1990), related and supporting industries mean the presence or absence of the internationally competitive suppliers and other related industries in the country. Porter's concept of related and supporting industries emphasizes more on the industry infrastructure (or physical infrastructure such as transportation and communication services). However, local living environment should also be an important concern, particularly, when MNCs send their own managers and employees to the host countries. Hence, related industries incorporate two sub-factors, industry infrastructure and living environment. Industry infrastructure comprises six composite indices and living environment, five composite indices (see Table 7.5).

Table 7.3.   Criteria of Factor Conditions

Sub-Factor		Criteria	Explanation	Data Type	Data Source
Basic	1.1.1	Annual salary	Compensation for manufacturing workers	Hard	IMD
	1.1.2	Labor force	Million people	Hard	WB
	1.1.3	Working hours	Weekly	Hard	ILO
	1.1.4	Natural resource endowment	Oil & natural gas production (% of market share)	Hard	CIA
	1.1.5	Land area	1000 ha	Hard	UN
	1.1.6	Land per capita	Land area/population	Hard	UN
	1.1.7	Rental price	(1) Apartment rent: 3-room apartment monthly rent in major cities (USD) (2) Office rent: Total occupation cost (USD/sq. m per year)	Hard	IMD
Advanced	1.2.1	Labor force with tertiary education	Percentage of total labor force	Hard	WB
	1.2.2	Researchers	Researchers in R&D per million inhabitants	Hard	WB
	1.2.3	Journal articles	Total number of scientific and technical journal articles.	Hard	WB
	1.2.4	Journal articles per capita	Scientific and technical journal articles per 1,000 inhabitants	Hard	WB

Business context (or Firm Strategy, Structure, and Rivalry) is the condition in the country on how firms are structured, organized, managed, and the nature of competition as well (Porter, 1990). Hence, the factor of business context is composed of firm strategy, organizational structure, and competition. Firm strategy is evaluated by three criteria; organizational structure is assessed by four; and competition is assessed by three criteria (see Table 7.6).

The role of government can influence the four determinants of the diamond model either positively or negatively through government policy

Table 7.4. Criteria of Demand Conditions

Sub-Factor		Criteria	Explanation	Data Type	Data Source
Size	2.1.1	GDP	Billion USD	Hard	WB
	2.1.2	GDP growth index	GDP × GDP growth rate	Hard	WB
	2.1.3	Goods export	Million USD	Hard	WB
	2.1.4	Goods import	Million USD	Hard	WB
	2.1.5	Service: credit	Million USD	Hard	IMF
	2.1.6	Service: debit	Million USD	Hard	IMF
Quality	2.2.1	Information	The consumers are well informed of products	Soft	IPS
	2.2.2	Quality	The consumers are sensitive to the quality of products	Soft	IPS
	2.2.3	Health & environment	The consumers are sensitive to health and environmental issues	Soft	IPS
	2.2.4	New products	The consumers are sensitive to the new products	Soft	IPS
	2.2.5	GDP per capita	USD	Hard	WB

(Porter, 1990). However, besides the government policy itself, the implementation capability of government is also highly associated with a nation's economic performance. Therefore, the factor of government is classified into regulations, incentives, and policy implementation structure. Regulations and incentives are two important types of government policy for attracting FDI, while policy implementation structure assesses government's capability to turn those policies into reality. Regulation is assessed by five criteria, incentives by four, and policy structure by three (see Table 7.7).

Data Process

A) Data Standardization
Since most of the criteria have different scales and units, in order to make them comparable, the Standard Deviation Method (SDM) is employed. This method measures the difference between an economy's performance,

Table 7.5.   Criteria of Related Industries

Sub-Factor		Criteria	Explanation	Data Type	Data Source
Industry Infrastructure	3.1.1	Transportation	Air/maritime/land transport	CI	UN, WB, KNSO
	3.1.2	Communication	Telephone & mobile phone/ internet	CI	WTI, IMD
	3.1.3	Finance	Financial risk/financial market sophistication	CI	PRSG, IPS
	3.1.4	Clustering	The number & cooperation level of local suppliers	CI	IPS
	3.1.5	Openness	Openness of cultural and physical economy	CI	IMD, AT Kearney
	3.1.6	Political stability	Political stability and absence of violence	Soft	WB
Living Environment	3.2.1	Education	Enrolment rate; education system; education market openness	CI	UNESCO, WB, IPS
	3.2.2	Medical service	Health expenditure; physicians; health infrastructure	CI	WB, IPS
	3.2.3	Healthy environment	Human Development Index	CI	UNDP
	3.2.4	Language capability	English & other languages	CI	ETS, IMD
	3.2.5	Social safety	Social safety net; public order, international homicides	CI	IPS, KNSO

Note: CI: Composite Index, KNSO: Korea National Statistical Office, WTI: World Telecommunication Indicators, PRSG: Political Risk Service Group, ETS: Educational Testing Services.

and its relative position in the final rankings (IMD, 2013). The formula for calculating the standardized score of the 55 criteria is as follows:

$$\frac{country\ score - sample\ minimum}{sample\ maximum - sample\ minimum} \times 100. \qquad (1)$$

In the above formula, sample maximum and sample minimum represent the highest and lowest scores in the sample of economies included in

Table 7.6. Criteria of Business Context

Sub-Factor		Criteria	Explanation	Data Type	Data Source
Strategy	4.1.1	Auditing & accounting practices	Auditing and accounting practices are adequately implemented in business	Soft	IMD
	4.1.2	Ethical practices	Ethical practices are implemented in companies	Soft	IMD
	4.1.3	Decision making	The entrepreneur's decision makings are swift and precise	Soft	IPS
Organization Structure	4.2.1	Labor & management	The relationship between labor and management is generally cooperative	Soft	IPS
	4.2.2	Shared value	Shared value is clear and well recognized in companies	Soft	IPS
	4.2.3	Corporate governance	Corporate governance is well organized to the market mechanism	Soft	IPS
	4.2.4	Firm restructuring	Firm restructuring is well conducted	Soft	IPS
Competition	4.3.1	Property right	Intellectual Property Rights Index	Hard	UNDP
	4.3.2	Equal treatment	Foreign and domestic firms are treated equally	Soft	IPS
	4.3.3	Competition	Rivalry among domestic firms is severe	Soft	IPS

the study. The country score refers to the relevant country's score of a specific criterion. Hence by using the formula, values of all economies for the above criteria are standardized to the index ranging from 0 to 100. In this index, a higher value represents a better performance, thereby a higher standardized score. For example, a country with the higher GDP per capita will have a higher standardized score, thereby ranked higher place. However, for some criteria, the higher value represents lower competitiveness. For example, the higher the corporate tax, the lower competitiveness the country has in attracting FDI. In this case, we use the following formula to ensure the higher value to represent a higher competitiveness:

$$100 - \left(\frac{country\ score - sample\ minimum}{sample\ maximum - sample\ minimum} \times 100 \right). \quad (2)$$

Table 7.7.   Criteria of Government

Sub-Factor		Criteria	Explanation	Data Type	Data Source
Regulation	5.1.1	Starting a business	Procedures, time, cost, and paid-in minimum capital to open a new business	Hard	WB
	5.1.2	Employing workers	Difficulty of hiring index, rigidity of hours index, difficulty of redundancy index and redundancy cost	Hard	WB
	5.1.3	Registering property	Procedures, time, and cost to transfer commercial real estate	Hard	WB
	5.1.4	Closing a business	Recovery rate in bankruptcy	Hard	WB
	5.1.5	Regulation intensity	Regulation intensity does not restrain the ability of companies to compete	Soft	IMD
Incentives	5.2.1	Effective personal income tax rate	Percentage of an income (GDP per capita)	Hard	WB
	5.2.2	Corporate tax rate on profit	Maximum tax rate (calculated on profit before tax)	Hard	WB
	5.2.3	Real personal income taxes	Real personal taxes do not discourage people from working or seeking advancement	Soft	IMD
	5.2.4	Real corporate taxes	Real corporate taxes do not discourage entrepreneurship	Soft	IMD
Policy Implementation Structure	5.3.1	Policy direction	Policy direction of the government is consistent	Soft	IMD
	5.3.2	Adaptability of government policy	Adaptability of government policy to changes in the economy is high	Soft	IMD
	5.3.3	Corruption	Corruption Perception Index	Soft	TI

B) *Aggregation*

Equal weights are given to all the criteria under the sub-factor, equal weights to the sub-factors under the factor, and equal weights to the factors under the overall index. Sub-factor rankings are derived from the sub-factor index, the average of the standardized criteria values. For example, the index of sub-factor 1.1 (basic factor conditions) is the average of seven standardized criteria values, and sub-factor 1.2 (advanced factor conditions) is the average of four standardized criteria values. The sub-factor rankings are determined by the sub-factor indices. The country with higher sub-factor index has higher ranking.

Next, the sub-factor indices are aggregated to calculate the factor indices and rankings. The factor index is the average of the sub-factor indices. There are two or three sub-factors under each factor, and hence each factor index is the average of its sub-factor indices. For example, "factor 1 index" is the average of sub-factor 1.1 and sub-factor 1.2 indices. Lastly, the standardized factor values are aggregated to determine the overall investment attractiveness index and ranking. The overall index is the average of four factor indices (see Figure 7.2).

C) *Three-Year Moving Average*

The moving average is commonly used by market analysts to understand the changing trend of stock price. As the stock price fluctuates wildly over time, it creates a smoother line by averaging the prices over a certain period of time (Hwa, 2007). A typical type of moving average is the simple moving average, which is to give equal weights for each datum value

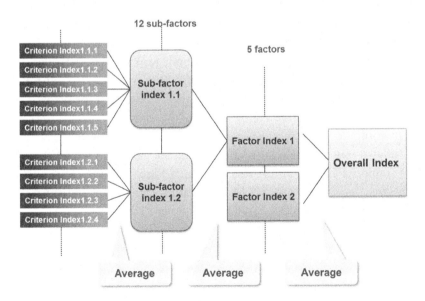

Figure 7.2   Integration and Calculating the Overall Index

(Gencay and Stengos, 1998). As this technique is useful to smooth out the volatility, we employ a three-year moving average for measuring the investment attractiveness.

7.3. Empirical Study

7.3.1. *Analysis of Korea's Business Environment*[4]

After the global financial crisis in 2008, the global flow of FDI displayed a significant decrease. Korea was also in a serious situation and it received several negative evaluations on its business environment from international media. In order to analyze the business environment of Korea,[5] the model (Figure 7.1) introduced in the previous section was utilized and compared for 35 economies, including OECD countries and other representative developing countries, such as Asia's newly industrializing economies and Brazil, Russia, India, China, and South Africa (BRICS). By ranking all the 35 economies for each criterion, sub-factor, and factor levels, Korea's relative positions in terms of its strengths and weaknesses among these economies were determined. For example, Korea was ranked 16th among the 35 economies in terms of the investment attractiveness. Within the 12 sub-factors, there are four sub-factors (advanced factor conditions, demand size, demand quality, and incentives) which are ranked higher than Korea's overall ranking,[6] while the other eight sub-factors have lower rankings than the overall ranking. In particular, the sub-factors rankings of organizational structure, regulations, and policy implementation structure are included in the bottom 30% (or below 24th among 35 economies) (see Figure 7.3).

By comparing the countries in the same competitive group, the OECD, we can also observe the relative distance or the gaps between the economies. Table 7.8 is an example that compares Korea and OECD countries in the areas of five factors and 12 sub-factors. The second and third col-

---

[4] This is based on the report published in Seoul National University (2009), conducted by Hwy-Chang Moon with the Ministry of Knowledge Economy of South Korea.

[5] It evaluated Korea's investment attractiveness in 2009. The data for measurement were the most recent data available at that time.

[6] The overall ranking is calculated using the overall index shown in Figure 7.2.

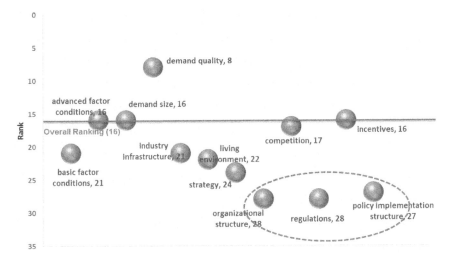

Figure 7.3 Structure of Korea's Investment Attractiveness

umns represent factor or sub-factor indices of OECD (average) and Korea. The fourth column refers to the score difference between Korea and OECD in each factor or sub-factor, and the fifth column indicates the relative percentage of the gap compared to the scores of OECD countries (see Table 7.8).

Compared with the OECD countries, Korea shows a relative weakness in all the four factors except for demand conditions, and Korea is particularly far behind in business context and the government. At the sub-factor level, Korea is relatively strong in demand quality and incentives, but weak in basic and advanced factor conditions, demand size, industry infrastructure, and competition. The areas of living environment, strategy, organizational structure, and government regulations display large weaknesses.

By combining the results of Figure 7.4 and Table 7.8, we can better understand Korea's strengths and weaknesses for its investment attractiveness. For example, in Figure 7.4, Korea shows competitive advantage in the advanced factor conditions, but when comparing with the OECD countries it shows a relative weakness. On the other hand, Korea ranks in a higher position in the area of government incentives compared with its overall ranking, and it also displays strong position relative to the average level of the OECD countries. This is to say, the assessments of Korea's investment attractiveness by the foreign media at that time emphasize more about

Table 7.8.   Comparison Between Korea and OECD Countries

	OECD (1)	Korea (2)	(2)–(1)	(2)–(1) / (1)
Factor Conditions	29.87	27.90	−1.96	−0.07
Basic	23.66	23.05	−0.61	−0.03
Advanced	36.07	32.75	−3.32	−0.09
Demand Conditions	38.64	44.02	5.38	0.14
Size	16.98	15.38	−1.59	−0.09
Quality	60.31	72.65	12.35	0.20
Related Industries	59.15	48.28	−10.87	−0.18
Industry infrastructure	51.80	45.70	−6.10	−0.12
Living environment	66.50	50.85	−15.65	−0.24
Business Context	52.91	36.74	−16.17	−0.31
Strategy	57.33	38.05	−19.28	−0.34
Organizational structure	49.45	25.21	−24.25	−0.49
Competition	51.95	46.97	−4.98	−0.10
Government	50.92	39.06	−11.85	−0.23
Regulations	65.09	45.65	−19.44	−0.30
Incentives	40.06	42.95	2.89	0.07
Policy implementation structure	47.60	28.60	−19.01	−0.40

Korea's weaknesses while neglecting its strengths. Therefore, an appropriate evaluation and analysis will not only provide useful information for the government to allocate the resources in certain strategic sectors, but also for foreign firms to make an appropriate decision in investing abroad.

The assessment model is not only helpful for analyzing a country's strengths and weaknesses of the investment environment, but also identifying the relationship (either competitive or cooperative) with other countries. Take Korea for example. Figure 7.4 shows Korea's relative competitiveness compared to Japan and China in terms of the investment attractiveness. If the numbers in the figure are closer to 100%, they represent that Korea has more similar level of attractiveness in that indicator with either Japan or China. If the numbers are larger than 100%, it means Korea is in a more attractive position. If the numbers are smaller than 100%, it signifies Korea's deficiency in that indicator. The larger gap implies a higher potential for cooperation than competition by exploiting each other's advantages.

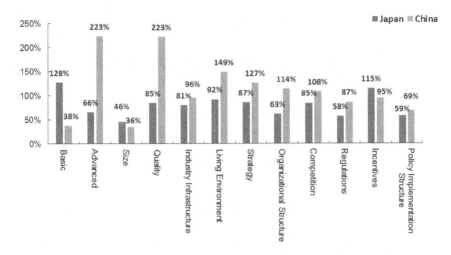

Figure 7.4 Comparison Between Korea and Other Asian Countries

Korea is often described as being "sandwiched" between Japan's competitive advantage in advanced technologies and China's competitive advantage in low cost. However, if we look into Figure 7.4, compared with Japan, Korea shows weaknesses in most areas except for basic factor conditions and incentives. Among the disadvantageous indicators, there is only one which shows the gap of less than 10% (living environment). Regarding China, Korea has more balanced distribution between superior and inferior indicators (six superior and six inferior indicators). Therefore, it implies that Korea has more room for cooperation with those two countries than being nutcrackered or sandwiched by those two countries. The cooperation of the three countries can thus promote synergistic effects in creating an attractive investment location in East Asia.

7.3.2. *Analysis of Azerbaijan's Business Environment*[7]

Azerbaijan has achieved a substantial economic growth since 1991 due to its rich endowment of natural resources, particularly oil and gas. However,

---

[7] The section is abstracted and modified from the research project which was published by the Institute for Industrial Policy Studies (IPS, 2012), organized by the IPS and supported by the Korean International Cooperation Agency (KOICA).

in an attempt to pursue more sustainable economic development, this country aimed to diversify its industry structure from oil to non-oil sectors. For achieving this goal, attracting foreign investment is crucial for importing technology, capital and management skills, and thereby diversifying industry structures to non-oil sectors.

In order to analyze the business environment of Azerbaijan and provide strategic guidelines for improving its business environment, this study employs a comprehensive analytical model (see Table 7.9) for evaluating Azerbaijan and its nine neighboring countries. The framework includes eight determinants — four physical factors (input conditions,[8] demand conditions, related industries, and business contexts) and four human factors (workers, government, entrepreneurs, and professionals). The framework is similar to the one (the extended diamond model) introduced in the previous section for assessing the business environment of Korea.

The framework used in assessing Azerbaijan's investment attractiveness, is modified from Porter's diamond model by distinguishing the physical and human factors for each determinant of the diamond model. For developing countries, because physical factors are not sufficiently developed, human factors play a particularly important role in attracting FDI and for national development by mobilizing and arranging the physical factors to gain international competitiveness (Cho, 1994; Cho and Moon, 2013a). At the initial stage of economic development, motivated, dedicated, and relatively well-educated people play a critical role in creating the competitive industries. The government allocates the scarce physical resources to the selected companies or some strategic industries to build the firm's capacity or industry competitiveness. The entrepreneurs play an important role in diversifying into new businesses which lead to the proliferation of related industries. Finally, the professionals (e.g., professional managers and engineers) help increase the productivity and product quality through various innovative activities (e.g., technology innovation).

In order to analyze the relative position of Azerbaijan's investment attractiveness, the country is compared with its neighboring countries. This is because neighboring countries share similar characteristics so global managers can assess which location serves better. For overall attractiveness

---

[8]Porter's factor conditions of the diamond model are renamed to input conditions.

Table 7.9. Variables for Azerbaijan's Investment Attractiveness

Physical Factors			Human Factors		
Factor	Sub-Factor	No. of Criteria	Factor	Sub-factor	No. of Criteria
Input Conditions	Energy resources	2	Workers	Quantity	4
	Other resources	4		Quality	4
Demand Conditions	Market size	4	Government	Transparency	4
	Market quality	3		Efficiency	3
Related Industries	Industry infrastructure	5	Entrepreneurs	Quantity	2
	Living environment	5		Social context	4
Business Context	Regulation	3	Professionals	Quantity	3
	Business culture	3		Social context	3
	Competition	4			

measured by the 8 criteria, Russia was ranked in the top of list, followed by Turkey, Kazakhstan, Azerbaijan, and Georgia out the 10 countries. Russia had the first rankings of four out of eight factors; Georgia had two; and Turkey and Azerbaijan only one respectively. The strong areas of these four countries are highlighted in the shaded cells in Table 7.10.

Figure 7.5 shows the competitiveness structure of Azerbaijan. Three factors including demand conditions, business context, and government are in the modest status. Two factors of input conditions and workers are ranked high. Azerbaijan's high performance in input conditions is mainly due to its high levels of production in oil and natural gas. The strength in workers is mainly derived from the quality of its workers. The other three factors of related industries, entrepreneurs, and professionals show particularly low competitiveness. Azerbaijan is lagging in related industries, particularly because of its poor performance in the living environment. For entrepreneurs and professionals, the common problem is attributed to the weaknesses in the personal competence of both entrepreneurs and professionals.

Among the inferior (both modest and low rankings) factors, demand conditions are not easy to improve in a short period, as it is determined by the size of population and sophistication of the market. Business context

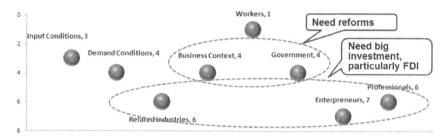

Figure 7.5   Azerbaijan's Competitiveness of Attractiveness Structure

and government, however, are more controllable and can be improved through government reforms. On the other hand, related industries, entrepreneurs, and professionals require large investments with both technology and capital.

The investment attractiveness model is also helpful to explain why some countries even without rich abundance of natural resources can be highly competitive in attracting FDI. The 10 countries are categorized into three groups depending on the level of endowment of natural resources and inward FDI actually received. Group A has both high levels of natural resources and inward FDI. Group B does not have rich endowment of natural resources, but attracts a high level of foreign investment. Group C has neither abundant natural resources nor foreign investment (see Figure 7.6).

If we look into specific components of assessment model of investment attractiveness, we can find that the countries in Group B are competitive in certain determinants of investment attractiveness. Turkey is competitive in demand conditions, related industries, business context, government, and professionals. Ukraine is competitive in related industries and professionals, whereas Georgia is competitive in business context and government (see Table 7.10).

7.4. Conclusion and Policy Implications

The global trend of government policies toward attracting FDI shows that there are more positive than negative policies. For example, in 2012 among the 86 policy measures, 75% are favorable to the investment liberalization and promotion, while the other 25% are FDI related regulations and restrictions (UNCTAD, 2013). In order to further induce FDI, governments

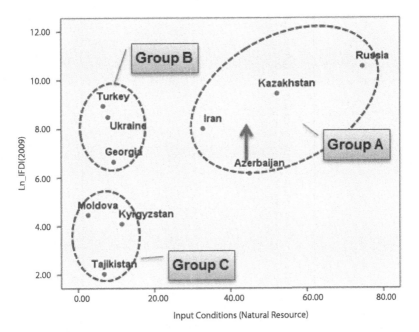

Figure 7.6   The Relationship Between Natural Resource and Inward FDI

Note: Ln_IFDI represents the natural logarithm of inward FDI; input conditions represent the score of the sub-factor of energy resources.

should look at all aspects of competitiveness variables. Considering the policy effectiveness and the limited resources, it would be better for the government to target a few most effective areas in different periods of time with different degrees of priority. For this, the framework of Term-Priority (TP) Matrix is suggested as shown in Figure 7.7 (Cho and Moon, 2013b).

Terms (*x*-axis) are classified into short, mid, and long. Priorities (*y*-axis) are classified into high, medium, and low. Each cell can be filled with policies that the government should do to improve the country's FDI environment. The classification standard is flexible depending on the objective of policy-makers. In general, the areas that are more related to public sectors are placed in the short term, and those more related to private sectors in the longer term, as the public sectors are more controllable by the government than private sectors. The level of priority (*y*-axis) is determined by the correlation between criterion of evaluation and the objective of policy-makers. Therefore, the policies in a shorter term with a higher priority are displayed in the upper-left triangle. The TP Matrix will

Table 7.10.   Overall and Factor Rankings

Country	Overall	Input Conditions	Demand Conditions	Related Industries	Business Context	Workers	Government	Entrepreneurs	Professionals
Russia	1	1	3	1	7	2	7	1	1
Turkey	2	9	1	2	2	8	2	3	2
Kazakhstan	3	2	2	8	3	3	3	5	4
Azerbaijan	4	3	4	6	4	1	4	7	6
Georgia	5	6	7	7	1	5	1	4	7
Iran	6	4	5	5	10	10	8	2	5
Ukraine	7	7	6	3	9	7	10	9	3
Moldova	8	10	8	4	6	9	5	8	8
Kyrgyzstan	9	5	9	9	5	6	9	6	10
Tajikistan	10	8	10	10	8	4	6	10	9

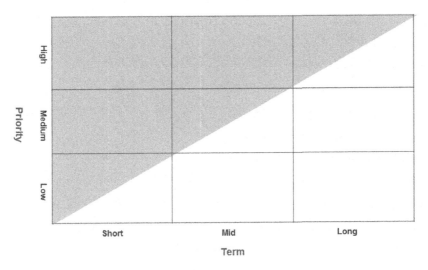

Figure 7.7 TP Matrix
Source: Cho and Moon (2013b).

thus show a comprehensive yet succinct list of policy prescriptions in an organized way.

For example, Figure 7.8 illustrates the TP Matrix presented to the Korean Ministry of Knowledge Economy for suggesting to enhance Korea's investment attractiveness. The indicators in each cell represent Korea's weaknesses. As shown in Figure 7.8, weaknesses of regulation, competition, policy implementation structure, and incentives are mostly related to the government sector, hence they are placed in the short term. On the other hand, the weaknesses of advanced factor conditions, industry infrastructure, and living environment depend more on the involvement and performance of the private sector, hence they are classified in the long term. And the other weaknesses are assigned in the mid-term, which are almost equally related to the government sector and to the private sector. In order to define the levels of importance of these policy variables, we calculated the correlation between the amount of inward FDI and each determinant. Then we categorized the sub-factors in each term into three priorities (high, medium, and low) using the Cluster Analysis.[9]

---

[9] Cluster Analysis is a frequently used classification technique for categorizing the observation into similar groups. In this chapter, we utilized the *K*-means clustering method for classification.

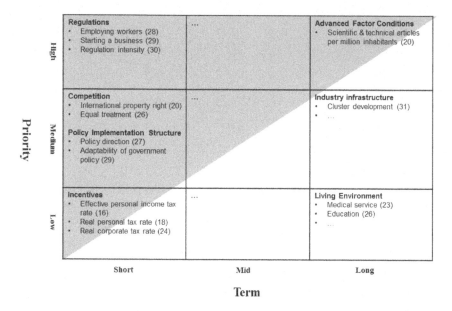

Figure 7.8   TP Matrix: Korea

Notes: 1) Numbers in the parentheses indicate the rankings of the criteria under each sub-factor. 2) This matrix is abstracted and modified with some deletions from the project report. This figure is for illustration, so for each cell, not all items are shown. The omitted items are marked with "...".

With a similar methodology, the TP matrix for the case of Azerbaijan is constructed. The term is classified into three periods, including short, mid, and long. The priority is divided into low, medium, and high, according to the correlation between the sub-factors and the GDP per capita.

As shown in Figure 7.9, the factors in the short run are government regulation policies, such as improving government transparency and efficiency, creating a business friendly environment, and strengthening the social context of both professionals and entrepreneurs. They are relatively easy for the government to change through a series of policy reform. In the mid-term, firms' business culture and competition and some other sub-factors are highlighted. These factors require commitment of both the government and private sectors. Finally, industry infrastructure, living environment, and the quantity of professionals and entrepreneurs are placed in the long run.

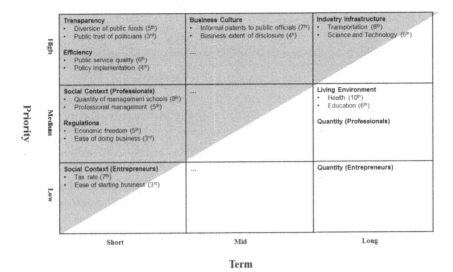

Figure 7.9   TP Matrix: Azerbaijan

Notes: 1) Numbers in the parentheses indicate the ranking of the criteria under each sub-factor. 2) This matrix is abstracted and modified with some deletions from the project report. This figure is for illustration, so for each cell, not all items are shown. The omitted items are marked with "…".

Appendix

Table A.1.   The Ease of Doing Business Index: 10 Determinants

Determinants	Contents
1. Starting a business	All procedures officially required to start up a business, the time and cost to complete these procedures, as well as the paid-in minimum capital requirement.
2. Dealing with construction permits	All procedures required for a business in the construction industry to build a warehouse.
3. Getting electricity	All procedures required for a business to obtain a permanent electricity connection and supply for a standardized warehouse.
4. Registering property	All procedures necessary for a business (buyer) to purchase a property from another business (seller) and to transfer the property title to the buyer's name.
5. Getting credit	The legal rights of borrowers and lenders with respect to secured transactions through one set of indicators and the sharing of credit information through another.
6. Protecting investors	The strength of minority shareholder protections against directors' misuse of corporate assets for personal gain.
7. Paying taxes	The taxes and mandatory contributions that a medium-size company must pay in a given year as well as measures of the administrative burden of paying taxes and contributions.
8. Trading across borders	The time and cost (excluding tariffs) associated with exporting and importing a standardized cargo of goods by sea transport.
9. Enforcing contracts	The efficiency of the judicial system in resolving a commercial dispute.
10. Resolving insolvency	The time, cost and outcome of insolvency proceedings involving domestic entities.

Source: The Ease of Doing Business (Methodology), http://www.doingbusiness.org/methodology.

Table A.2.   The Index of Economic Freedom: 10 Components

Determinants	Contents
Rule of Law	
1. Property rights	The extent to which a country's legal framework allows individuals to freely accumulate private property.
2. Freedom from corruption	Derived primarily from Transparency International's Corruption Perceptions Index (CPI).
Government Size	
3. Fiscal freedom	The burden of taxes that reflects both marginal tax rates and the overall level of taxation.
4. Government spending	The burden imposed by government expenditures, including consumption by the state and all transfer payments related to various entitlement programs.
Regulatory Efficiency	
5. Business freedom	The efficiency of government regulation of business.
6. Labor freedom	Various aspects of the legal and regulatory framework of a country's labor market.
7. Monetary freedom	Price stability with an assessment of price controls.
Open Markets	
8. Trade freedom	The extent of tariff and non-tariff barriers that affect imports and exports of goods and services.
9. Investment freedom	No constraints on the flow of investment capital.
10. Financial freedom	Banking efficiency as well as a measure of independence from government control and interference in the financial sector.

Source: The Wall Street Journal and The Heritage Foundation (Methodology), http://www.heritage.org/index/book/methodology.

Table A.3.   18-Month Risk Factors and 5-Year Risk Factors

Item	Factors
18-Month Forecast	Turmoil, equity restriction, Operations restrictions, Taxation discrimination, Repatriation restrictions, Exchange controls, Tariff barriers, Other import barriers, Payment delays, Fiscal and monetary expansion, Labor policies, Foreign debt
5-Year Forecast	Investment restrictions, Trade restrictions, Domestic economic problems, International economic problems, turmoil

Source: PRS methodology, http://www.prsgroup.com/PRS_Methodology.aspx.

Table A.4.   ICRG: 22 Factors

Political Risk	Economic Risk	Financial Risk
1. Government stability	1. GDP per head	1. Foreign debt as a percentage of GDP
2. Socioeconomic conditions	2. Real GDP growth	
3. Investment profile	3. Annual inflation rate	2. Foreign debt service as a percentage of exports of goods and services
4. Internal conflict	4. Budget balance as a percentage of GDP	
5. External conflict	5. Current account as a percentage of GDP	3. Current account as a percentage of exports of goods and services
6. Corruption		
7. Military in politics		
8. Religious tensions		4. Net international liquidity as months of import cover
9. Law and order		
10. Ethnic tensions		
11. Democratic accountability		
12. Bureaucracy quality		5. Exchange rate stability

Source: ICRG Methodology, http://www.prsgroup.com/ICRG_Methodology.aspx.

Table A.5. Determinants of Inward FDI Potential Index

Determinants	Proxy Indicators
Market attractiveness	• Size of the market (GDP) • Purchasing power (per capita GDP) • Growth potential of the market (real GDP growth rate)
Availability of low-cost labor and skills	• Unit labor cost (hourly compensation and labor productivity) • Size of manufacturing workforce (existing skill base)
Presence of natural resources	• Exploitation of resources (value of fuels and ores exports) • Agricultural potential (availability of arable land)
Enabling infrastructure	• Transport infrastructure (km of road per 100 km^2 of land area, percentage of paved roads in total, rail lines total route-km, liner shipping connectivity index) • Energy infrastructure (electric power consumption) • Telecom infrastructure (telecom lines per 100 inhabitants, mobile cellular subscriptions per 100 inhabitants, fixed broadband Internet subscribers per 100 inhabitants)

Source: UNCTAD (2012).

Table A.6. Comparison of the Three Competitiveness Reports

	WCY 2013 (IMD)	GCR 2013–2014 (WEF)	NCR 2013 (IPS)
No. of countries	60	148	62
Competiveness model	4 factors 20 sub-factors 333 criteria	3 factors 12 sub-factors 114 criteria	8 factors 16 sub-factors 116 criteria
	4 Factors • Economic performance • Government efficiency • Business efficiency • Infrastructure	3 Factors • Basic requirements • Efficiency enhancers • Innovation and sophistication factors	8 Factors • Factors conditions • Demand conditions • Related industries • Business context • Workers • Politicians & bureaucrats • Entrepreneurs • Professionals
Data base	Hard data (2/3) Soft data (1/3)	Hard data (1/3) Soft data (2/3)	Hard data (1/2) Soft data (1/2)

Chapter 8

Entry Mode Choices: From Market Failure to Three Considerations[1]

Summary

We have examined why and where firms invest in previous chapters. Then, how do firms enter foreign locations? There are various types of entry modes. The distinction between these choices was initially explained by the transaction cost theory. However, based on the assumptions behind the ownership-location-internalization (OLI) paradigm and the imbalance theory, this chapter introduces three other criteria in choosing the entry modes of foreign direct investment (FDI). They are market failure, complementarity, and locational factors. With an increasing interdependence of firms, furthermore, foreign market entry mode should be understood from an ecological perspective. It is important to know how firms should configure and coordinate their value activities across national borders through firm networks, rather than looking into one-to-one multinational corporation (MNC) relationship with a local firm or a host country. The ecological perspective on foreign entry modes, thus, is presented as an extension to three variables, and draws implications in creating sustainable competitive advantages across national borders.

8.1. Externalization vs. Internalization

Foreign country entry mode is defined as institutional arrangement that allows firms to enter a foreign country with their products, technology,

---

[1]This chapter is prepared by Sohyun Yim in consultation with Professor Hwy-Chang Moon.

Table 8.1. Different Types of Entry Modes

Externalization	Internalization
• Trade (intra-industry trade, inter-industry trade) • Contract production (outsourcing) • Licensing (franchising)	• Strategic alliances (minority stakes) • Joint venture • Wholly-owned subsidiary (greenfield investment and M&A)

human skills, management, and other resources (Root, 1987; Calof, 1993; Rasheed, 2005). In general, foreign entry modes are distinguished into two: externalization or internalization (see Table 8.1). Externalization is a contract-based entry mode such as trade, contract production, and licensing. Internalization accompanies higher control and risks associated with the investing firm's resource commitments (i.e., equity) and it is conducted in the form of strategic alliances, joint ventures, or wholly-owned subsidiaries.

8.1.1. *Externalization*

Trade is a transfer of final or intermediary goods and services across national boundaries. The production is mainly done in home country and transactions take place in international market. No resources, controls, or risks are exchanged with a foreign country.[2]

Contract production is a form of outsourcing and engaging in partnerships with other firms that can do the work "better." This can be understood in terms of division of labor or specialization based on firm's comparative advantages. If a firm believes the other firm performs better

---

[2] Here, we adopt definitions of control and resource commitment presented by Hill, Hwang, and Kim (1990). *Control* is defined as the authority over operational and strategic decision making and *resource commitment* is referred to dedicated assets that cannot be redeployed to alternative uses without cost (loss of value). Resource commitment may be tangible like equity or physical plant, or intangible like management or technological know-how (as we have examined from resource-based view (RBV)). A higher resource commitment also means setting up a high exit barrier of foreign investment (sunk cost that cannot be recovered) because it inhibits firm's flexibility to environmental changes.

than itself, it lets the others do the work. This is different from licensing as there is no transfer of firm assets or resources.

Licensing is a transfer or a sale of knowledge and know-how to other firm in an external market. A firm with proprietary assets gives the right to engage in value activities to another firm, in exchange of a lump sum payment or royalty fee per unit sales based on the terms set out in the licensing contract. This is done between independent parties of the licensor and the licensee. The licensor does not have equity investment with the licensee, so it has no resource commitment over the foreign (licensee) firm.

Externalization is a transaction with contract (Rasheed, 2005). Thus, externalization is not counted as FDI which accompanies a certain level of administrative control over foreign operations.[3] FDI is a form of internalizing foreign market. By transferring their firm-specific resources, MNCs internalize foreign transactions to a varying degree.

8.1.2. *Internalization*

FDI entails investments and resource commitments, so it is an equity or control-based contract. Depending on the degree of equity (ownership) or control over foreign operations, the entry modes vary. Let's take a look at each entry mode.

First, *minority stakes* are when a firm is holding not large, but just a certain level of ownership and control over another firm. As the investing firm holds some equity, this accompanies taking risks to the level of the equity ownership. Holding minority stakes is often preferred in cases where the two competing firms need to strengthen their cooperation on operational issues and strategy (Schmid and Grosche, 2013).

This is similar to *strategic alliance* as it does not necessarily involve equity investments (Moon, 1997), rather firms cooperate in terms of exchanging, sharing, and co-developing products, technologies, and services (Gulati, 1998). As opposed to unilateral and hierarchical management of

---

[3] According to the International Monetary Fund (IMF), FDI is usually defined as an investment that holds 10% or more of the equity of a firm abroad, enough for the investor to have some influence on its management.

the investing firm, strategic alliance entails a more collateral and mutual relationship between partnering firms. The term, however, is often used broadly where scholars do not distinguish it from the minority stakes and joint venture. It could be sometimes used in terms of outsourcing.

A *joint venture* is defined as a contractual agreement in which the participating parties agree to share major decision-making. The profits and losses are based on their equity investment range. Thus, the extent of equity holdings is unclear and is not distinguishable from the minority stakes and strategic alliances. Here, we distinguish joint venture from strategic alliance by whether the investing firm has a substantial control or equity over the other party or not. If not, it is considered as a strategic alliance, and if yes, it is considered as a joint venture.[4]

A *wholly-owned subsidiary* is a 100% investment made by the investing firm in a foreign location, which has full control and resource commitments over its business operations. In this case, the control over day-to-day operations and certain strategic decisions may be delegated to the foreign subsidiary, but the ultimate control always resides in the MNC headquarters (Moon, 1997). The wholly-owned subsidiary is either a newly established venture (i.e., greenfield investment) or a firm that is acquired and has become a subsidiary of the investing firm (i.e., mergers and acquisitions).

8.2. Explanatory Variables[5]

Theoretical foundations of FDI were examined from various perspectives: from market failure to business theories (see Chapter 2). Entry mode choices can also be analyzed in the same context. As the FDI theories have been initially developed from market failure perspectives, market failure

---

[4] The distinction between minority stakes and joint ventures was considered to be the amount of equity involvement, which has become less compelling nowadays, as equity investments can be carried out in complex ways and their actual control and management involvement may differ from their actual stake holdings (Schmid and Grosche, 2013). Sometimes they are distinguished by the amount of pooled resources and assets, which may be even more difficult to measure. Yet, if we were to compare the level of risks and control involved, we can see that, in general, they are higher in joint ventures than in minority stakes.

[5] This part was abstracted and extended from Moon's (1997) article.

was the frequently utilized variable in analyzing entry modes. However, as an extension to the OLI paradigm and as suggested in the imbalance theory, asset augmentation or complementarity has also been important in choosing the entry mode, together with another consideration, i.e., where the assets are embedded in. Thus, an integrated framework can be illustrated, combining three variables — market failure, location factor, and complementarity.

8.2.1. *Market Failure*

FDI theory is based on the market failure assumption (e.g., Anderson and Gatignon, 1986). Structural market failure is due to MNC's expansion to foreign locations through exploiting its monopolistic assets. If there is no market that can fairly evaluate the value of the monopolistic asset (ownership advantage) in host countries, the MNC would establish its own firm to fully appropriate its value and internalize the foreign market. This is why earlier studies of FDI based on structural market failures considered only the wholly-owned subsidiary for foreign market entry mode (Moon, 1997).

In business theories, the monopolistic assets can be interpreted from the resource-based view (RBV) — unequal distribution of resources across firms. Certain resources are hard to be attained and thus become the sources of sustainable competitive advantage (e.g., Wernerfelt, 1984; Barney, 1991). If the resources are hard to be codified or specialized, they are also hard to be transferred to other firms (Kogut and Zander, 1993). Thus, resource specificity affects choices of entry modes, where hard-to-codify resources usually entail a higher control and management of the firm (Teece, 1986a). The higher the market failure is, the more the firms internalize inter-country transactions. It is because when a larger geographical and cultural distance is considered as "costs" coming from unfamiliarity, the costs occur from not only transactions, but also from coordination of resources across unfamiliar business environments. Thus, higher costs or risks make firms have a higher degree of integration or control (Williamson, 1991).

Market failure is understood in terms of costs and risks associated with international transactions. Cost refers to inefficiencies in the transaction processes such as information searching, bargaining, operations, and executions. Risk comes from the dissipation of technological know-how, import barriers, global strategy, and lack of trust (Moon, 1997). These risks emanate from bounded rationality, opportunism, asset specificity, and from a lack of efficient institutions for transactions (Williamson, 1979). Thus, costs and risks associated with these features can all be understood under the context of "market failure."

8.2.2. *Location Factors*

Until the OLI paradigm was introduced, location-specific resources had not been distinguished from firm-specific advantages. It is because the primary shift from trade to FDI was mainly explained by market failure and exploiting ownership advantages. Various entry modes were thus not considered and could not be satisfactorily explained. With the evolution of Dunning's OLI paradigm, finding the optimal geographical location for FDI has become a critical issue, in addition to market failure. Among various locations, some countries were more attractive than others. Some locations also have resources that MNC's home country does not have. Thus, MNCs choose certain locations over others to exploit specific locational advantages.

Although locational advantage has been specified as the second variable for FDI, Dunning still could not satisfactorily explain the difference between wholly-owned subsidiary and joint venture. This is because the conventional type of FDI is mainly downward, from developed to developing countries. In this world of conventional FDI, firms in developing countries do not possess any significant firm-specific advantages that MNCs from developed countries have. Therefore, entry modes such as a joint venture were not included in the analysis (Moon, 1997).

When MNCs enter host countries, they exploit either local firm-specific resources or country-specific resources. For example, if the MNC wants to have access to local firm's knowledge and technology, it is seeking local firm-specific assets. If the MNC wants to exploit natural resources and unskilled workers, it is seeking country-specific assets. However, if the MNC is partnering with a local firm that has a better capability of exploiting these country-specific advantages than other firms in that country, the partnership then aims to seek local firm's firm-specific assets (Moon, 1997).

Although Dunning mainly focused on country-specific assets, the notion of firm-specific asset was mentioned by Hymer (1976). He stated that firms need to form networks with local firms in order to overcome costs of foreignness. Yet, he did not delve into different types of entry modes. Other scholars, on the other hand, pointed out the importance of firm-specific advantages, where finding an appropriate partner can actually provide a better solution to the problems arising from opportunism and bounded rationality (Beamish and Banks, 1987). Thus, the distinction between firm-specific and country-specific locational factors, by incorporating the concept of the imbalance that explains the optimality of firm's asset-portfolio, can better explain both the upward and downward FDI as well as why firms are choosing joint ventures as opposed to setting up wholly-owned subsidiaries. The imbalance theory also leads to an addition of one more variable, complementarity, to explain various entry modes.

8.2.3. *Complementarity*

FDI has increasingly played a significant role in search of competitiveness and the development of new advantages. Although earlier works on FDI did not incorporate complementarity, scholars emphasized that firms seek location advantages to augment and enhance their current competitive assets (e.g., Teece, 1992). As firms face an imbalance in their assets as they grow (Penrose, 1956; 1959), for a sustainable growth, firms constantly seek a balance between the exploitation of existing resources and the development of new ones (Wernerfelt, 1984; March, 1991).

Complementarity can be understood side by side with resource pooling and co-specialization. Firms ally in order to acquire other's know-how or resources. When two sets of resources are co-specialized, the return that can be derived from the use of one set depends on how the other set is used simultaneously or sequentially (Teece, 1986a). The combination of IBM's resource for making personal computers and Microsoft's resources for developing operating systems are examples of co-specialization (Chi, 1994). The outcome of resource pooling or co-specialization depends on firms' complementary capabilities (absorptive capacity and combinative capabilities).

Co-specialization and complementing comparative disadvantages are already examined in various contexts and are increasingly prevalent in business practices (see Chapter 4). For example, Indonesian firms invested abroad to complement management expertise, exports quality, and costs relative to other competitors at home (Lecraw, 1993). Complementarity is thus an essential variable to explain the growth of the firm and different types of FDI.

8.3. Entry Mode Framework

Most of the existing studies have tried to explain a few foreign country entry modes with just one or two aspects of the three explanatory variables. However, all these three explanatory variables are needed to explain various types of entry modes. The integrated framework gives six different types of entry modes.

8.3.1. *An Integrated Framework for Entry Mode Choices*

Trade and licensing are considered as the two major means of externalization. The distinction between the two did not receive much attention because externalization is possible only when market failure is low. In other words, they were not considered in the studies of FDI as the conventional FDI theory deals principally with one variable i.e., market failure.

There are two kinds of trade: inter-industry trade and intra-industry trade. Inter-industry trade refers to a trade pattern predicted by the Heckscher–Ohlin–Samuelson (HOS) model. A country is likely to produce and export abundant-factor goods and import scarce-factor goods. Intra-industry trade, on the other hand, takes place between countries with similar factor endowments, within an industry consisting of differentiated but similar products with similar technology (Moon, 1997). This is based on Linder's country similarity theory that a country exports goods to countries with similar tastes and income levels, so this theory focuses only on the demand side (Cho and Moon, 2013a).

Subsequent scholars, however, extended Stefan Linder's theory to include the concept of "close substitute products" (Dixit and Norman, 1980) in trade between countries with "close factor proportions" (Helpman, 1981) which considers both supply and demand sides. For example, in automobile industry, the US exports relatively large cars and Japan exports small cars. This is contrast to HOS model, arguing that the motivation of trade is due to different industry structure, i.e., complementarity.

The difference between licensing and trade is that trade is seeking country-specific advantages (i.e., host country's market) and licensing is seeking local firm's advantages (e.g., manufacturing and sales capabilities). Yet, licensing has low complementarity as the licensee firm does similar activities as the licensor firm.

On the other hand, the distinction between externalization and internalization lies in the degree of market failure. The higher is the market failure, the more the firm will try to internalize the market. A higher internalization or integration often accompanies a higher equity investment over the local firms.[6] Thus, strategic alliance will be chosen in the case of low market failure and joint venture in high market failure.

Wholly-owned subsidiary and joint venture, the means of FDI, are taken place in high market failure to complement their imbalances in their asset portfolio. The distinction between the two can be made based on the location factors. Wholly-owned subsidiary is to complement with country-specific advantages such as cheap labor and natural resource availability. On the other hand, forming a joint venture, compared to a wholly-owned subsidiary, is to seek another firm's resources.

With three explanatory variables, as shown in Table 8.2, six types of entry modes can be explained. With only one variable of market failure, conventional FDI scholars explained that a joint venture is a quasi-hierarchy transaction structure. Now, with the two additional variables, we can explain easily the various types of entry modes. For example, strategic alliance is preferred in a lower market failure to the joint venture, and when there is a high complementarity between the firm and its partner. This framework can also give managerial implications by suggesting three steps for using the three explanatory variables in choosing an appropriate entry mode. These steps are illustrated in Figure 8.1. First, the MNC has to decide why it is entering the foreign location, i.e., whether it is to complement firm-specific resource or country-specific resource (location factor). Then, for each case, can determine the degree of market failure in the host country

---

[6]This is under the assumption that the amount of equity investment equates the level of control over another firm, i.e., a higher equity stake, a higher control over another firm.

Table 8.2. Entry Modes and Explanatory Variables

		Market Failure		Complementarity	
		High	Low	High	Low
Country-specific advantage	Inter-industry trade		X	X	
	Intra-industry trade		X		X
	Wholly-owned subsidiary	X		X	
Firm-specific advantage	Joint venture	X		X	
	Strategic alliance		X	X	
	Licensing		X		X

Source: Moon (1997).

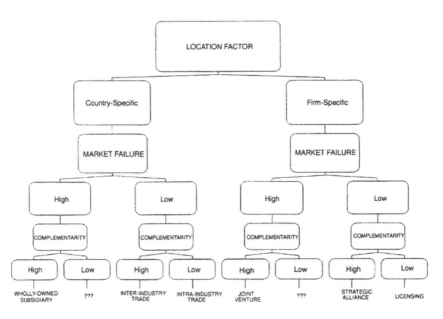

Figure 8.1 Flow Chart for Manager's Choice on Entry Modes
Source: Moon (1997).

(market failure). Based on the complementarity of the resources, the manager can choose the final entry mode.

There are two cases which are marked with "???" which mean no business or termination of contract. For example, in the case of joint venture, increasing transfers of proprietary resources among parties over time imply that their identities and unique domains may gradually shift from being complementary to being undistinguished (Ring and Van de Ven, 1994). As the complementarity becomes low from the evolutionary perspective, the contracting parties will rethink the terms of the relationship and make a strategic move by terminating the existing joint venture relationships.

Similarly, when an MNC has a wholly-owned subsidiary, the country-specific factors may change over time to an unfavorable situation. An increase in low-skilled workers' wage or a depletion of natural resources will reduce complementarity for the MNC in the host country. Thus, as the complementarity becomes lower, the firm will either choose to pull back or relocate its business elsewhere. Thus, the integrated framework of entry mode is useful in explaining the evolutionary perspective on entry modes. It also explains various types of entry modes, whereas most of the existing studies on entry modes remain static and explain just a few types of entry modes.

8.3.2. *Application of the Integrated Model to Automobile Industry*[7]

In order to illustrate how the integrated model of entry mode choices can be applied to the real world cases, this part presents the cases of Korean and Japanese automobile firms in India. As the Indian market was liberalized in 1991, the GDP growth was substantial along with the inflow of FDI to India. In order to boost economic growth, the Ministry of External Affairs of India targeted the automotive sector as a core strategic industry for economic development, as its substantial spillover effects on related sectors can be large.

The two prominent automakers, Maruti-Suzuki from Japan and Hyundai Motor from Korea were both successful in the Indian market. They ranked first and second respectively, in 2013. The difference between those two companies is that Suzuki Motors formed a joint venture with an existing automaker, Maruti Udyog Limited (MUL) and Hyundai Motor established a wholly-owned subsidiary upon entering the Indian market.

According to the model presented above, both joint venture and wholly-owned subsidiary take place where there are high market failure

---

[7]This part was abstracted and extended from Moon and Kwon (2010).

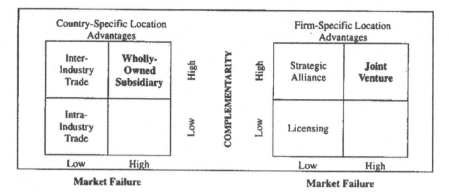

Figure 8.2   Entry Mode Explanatory Variables Between Joint Venture and Wholly-Owned Subsidiary
Sources: Moon (1997), Moon, and Kwon (2010).

and high complementarity with the location (see Figure 8.2). The difference is where the complementarity comes from. The joint venture is to seek firm-specific resources and the wholly-owned subsidiary is to seek country-specific resources.

Suzuki formed a joint venture with the local firm in order to complement its weaknesses in capabilities to start a new venture in a foreign country and to access high skilled managers. Hyundai Motor, on the other hand, was seeking a large pool of labor force who could speak English to communicate with workers sent from Korea, in order to overcome its saturated market and increasing wage level at home. India's strong Information Technology (IT) infrastructure also helped Hyundai Motor to easily utilize its locational resources. Thus, Suzuki and Hyundai Motor chose different entry modes in entering the same Indian market.

8.4. Extension of the Integrated Model: From Entry Mode to Global Ecosystem

The integrated model is very useful and comprehensive in explaining various entry modes. Yet, as firm alliances and networks have become increasingly complicated, the characteristics of entry modes have also been changed. First, the level of ownership and control over another firm have not necessarily been equated. Sometimes, a firm with a higher equity investment has less control over another firm and vice versa. Sometimes, a licensing firm has a higher control over the licensee firm than firms that have formed joint ventures, but operates independently.

Second, firm strategies affect entry mode decisions and the relationship with foreign subsidiaries. If firms pursue a multi-domestic strategy over their foreign subsidiaries or partnering firms, they require less interactions and control, and if firms pursue global strategy, they tend to have a higher control to standardize their operations (Bartlett, 1986; Harzing, 2002). Although licensing and outsourcing were conventionally considered to entail no risks and control over the other firm, the licensor has increasingly been charged with unexpected risks, misbehavior, or an illegal act by the licensee or "outsourced" firms. For example, when Nike's outsourced factories in developing countries were accused of child labor and bad working conditions, the incident badly tarnished and hurt Nike's performances (Nisen, 2013). Another example is the case of Apple. When its production factory in China was revealed to have unfavorable working conditions for its workers, Apple's image was severely hurt (Adams, 2012; Harris, 2012).

Thus, we need to expand our view on firm operations to an entire value chain. The behavior of one firm has an effect on other firms' activities and it is crucial to maintain a balance across the entire value chain activities. No firms can survive on their own value chain and firms grow in cooperation with other firms (e.g., Yim, 2013). They create competitive advantages together. Rather than having a unique resource set, finding a unique alliance-portfolio across national borders has increasingly become the key to creating sustainable competitive advantages (e.g., Dyer and Singh, 1998). Firms ally in one way or the other across value chain activities and how they manage them can give a useful picture of global business strategies of MNCs.

There are variations in how firms form networks and cooperate with each other. In many cases, firms exchange knowledge and co-develop technologies without any equity investments involved. Firms try to create values across national borders and increase efficiency. Firm alliances also include a more complex forms such as research and development (R&D) consortia and patent pooling. Firms utilize these methods to establish industry standardization and enhance their position in the marketplace.

MNCs either form networks with the country or local firms and balance out their value chain activities across borders (Yim, 2013). Firms configure their value chain activities abroad in different locations and they integrate or give independence to local operations based on the nature of firm interactions. Firms exploit and complement resources from each region and add values throughout the entire business processes. Processing, learning, combining, and transforming resources and knowledge are critical parts of the value chain activities and are essential for firm sustainability. Thus, we adopt the terminology of global value chain (GVC) to better understand firm alliances.

The terminology of GVC is not new, but the scope of analysis has been very limited or skewed in the previous studies. Particularly, in trade studies, as value chain is often utilized to analyze the production processes such as trade value of intermediary goods versus the final goods, the analysis of value chain is limited to the management of supply chain or just upstream activities. The scope of GVC needs to be extended, because FDI studies look into what resources are exploited and complemented in each region throughout the entire GVC on a global basis.

Firms deploy their activities in locations and cooperate with other firms that can efficiently perform their jobs, and with those that can complement the resources they lack. They cooperate across national borders and across industry boundaries. The outcome of a firm is a continuous process of value-added activities. Thus, the boundary of a firm should be expanded from a single firm to an entire value chain of firm networks.

Firm networks are formed through either internalization or externalization processes, or through direct or indirect relationships. They can also be formed through geographical proximity. They transfer and exchange resources and knowledge mutually as the value chain activities have become "non-linear" compared to the traditional linear sequence activities of value chain (Rayport and Sviokla, 1995). In this respect, GVC should be regarded as an ecosystem, not a one-way process of value-added activities.

Then how should we understand the GVC from ecological perspective? The key aspect to firm cooperation is creating values together. Although firms may be in both competitive and cooperative relationships, they need to co-exist together to bring synergistic effects to the ecosystem. The more they bring in values, the more competitive the ecosystem becomes, and vice versa. The self-reinforcing mechanisms are thus critical in firm alliances, in order to most efficiently create mutual values and increase productivity among partnering firms.

Then what are the determinants for creating self-reinforcing mechanism for mutual value creation? When MNCs ally with local firms or enter foreign markets, they need to have compatibility with local partners as well as with the country-specific resources. It is not a matter of whether similar or different resources are pooled or not. It is a matter of how much firms can find compatibility among the resources and create unique values from resource combinations.

The compatible, yet heterogeneous combinations will bring added values to the firms, industries and the host country, and reduce market transaction costs. In conventional perspectives, FDI is regarded as to exploit only firm-specific resources, but collaborating with local partners with compatible capabilities can bring synergistic effects to the entire ecosystem. This leads to the second aspect for successful collaboration, i.e., the complementarity.

Complementarity can be understood in a similar context as why firms invest in foreign locations and choose different entry modes. Firms need to form alliances with complementary firms which can enhance firm's core competencies and at the same time complement their support and related activities in GVC. The synergistic impacts are brought by complementing their own disadvantages and also providing complements that competitors critically lack. In this way firms form an ecosystem where they can both benefit and contribute with their unique complementary resources which are compatible with other resources (through co-specialization).

The competitiveness of GVC can be further enhanced through finding unique and diverse sets of firm connectivity. Connectivity has been emphasized in the studies of GVC, yet they are focused more on physical connectivity such as well-developed transportation systems and other infrastructures. However, in addition to this physical connectivity, the competitiveness is affected by other factors such as the mechanism of firms to share and augment new resources intensively, and by forming platforms with other firms virtually. For example, Ford established a virtual work team of the best engineering designers and marketing talents around the world and moved key value chain activities to the virtual space (Rayport and Sviokla, 1995). Thus, the formation of a unique and diverse portfolio of firm connectivity spatially and/or virtually to access and distribute inputs and outputs has become the key to enhancing competitiveness of the GVC (Dyer and Singh, 1998; Rayport and Sviokla, 1995). Moreover, the host country may want MNCs to help local firms engage in diverse networks rather than to merely transfer firm resources. The newly formed networks for local firms will help them develop and sustain their growth. In the end, these networks will serve as the channel for new and diverse knowledge source.

In the past, the value creation was about delivering a unique experience by upgrading technology and key components. However, value creation has changed to providing efficient and user-friendly experience (i.e., commerciality) that does not necessarily come from superior or new technology. The advancement of technology may sometimes give more complications to the entire value chain as cooperating firms may not be able to learn and upgrade in a similar manner. The new technology might also not give much value to the customers by increasing learning and switching costs. This is to say that the development of a new technology can bring more values to technology advancement in the industry, than to the market or the end customers. That may in the end fail to prevail in the market. This is usually the case of venture firms; despite new high technology, they are not appealing in the market. Thus, as the industry has become more market-driven, it is important to enhance value creation by providing a portfolio of products that are tailored to the market needs, rather than just by depending on a few high technologies.

The four criteria presented here are based on creating mutual values between the MNCs and the host country, and also with (local) partnering firms (Yim, 2013). Although Yim (2013) looked into country-based location factors, this chapter extends this perspective by giving an implication that firms can form ecosystem-based business models to create values through exchanging firm-specific resources. In short, the four variables-compatibility, complementarity, connectivity, and commerciality, are useful in choosing an entry mode in foreign locations to build a competitive GVC from ecological perspective.

8.5. Conclusion

This chapter has given three key explanatory variables to distinguish different foreign entry modes. If market failure is low, firms will choose to externalize. When market failure is high, firms will internalize foreign markets. When complementarity is high with local firms' resources, MNCs will choose to form a joint venture. If complementarity is high with host country-specific resources, MNCs will establish a wholly-owned subsidiary.

Yet, as firms increasingly engage in complex and interdependent firm-relationships across their entire value chain activities, foreign country entry mode should be understood not only in terms of asset exploitation, but to find a balance across firm alliances and with the host country's needs. In the past, firms' entry mode was analyzed only in terms of an independent firm or one-to-one firm relationship. As firms become increasingly interdependent and operate in cooperation with other firms, the concept of GVC gives a better understanding of why and how firms engage in FDI. The ecological perspective of GVC gives great implications in how we understand a firm, an industry, and a national boundary. We can also infer how firms and nations can co-develop and upgrade through enhancing compatibility, complementarity, connectivity, and commerciality.

Chapter 9

Global Citizenship: From Responsibility to Opportunity

Summary

In the previous chapter, enhancing firm competitiveness through foreign direct investment (FDI) was examined from the ecosystemic view of firms participating in the global value chain (GVC). We now take a step further to analyze how multinational corporations (MNCs) can co-create values with the host and home countries for sustainable development of firms and societies. While social activities may still be taken as a burden that MNCs need to address in business activities, they can become the driving force for finding new business opportunities and at the same time for sustaining and enhancing competitiveness. For this purpose, in order to extend the perspective of corporate social responsibility (CSR), this chapter presents creating shared value (CSV) and corporate social opportunity (CSO) as important strategies for MNCs in engaging in FDI. CSO is to find business sustainability by co-creating values with the host countries, which enhances the relationship between the investing firm and invested countries. This concept and strategy of CSO can also provide useful implications for the successful operation of official development assistance (ODA) where MNCs' role has been increasingly important in recent years.

9.1. CSR in International Business

As firm's value chain activities have become more complex and extended, managing risks in business operations has become ever more critical and difficult. Not only does the firm increasingly face pressure to comply with the code of conduct in business operations, the level of restrictions and regulations has been heightened.[1] Without creating meaningful values to the host country as well as to the home country, MNCs have increasingly been losing legitimacy to invest abroad. Firms are nowadays required to bring other positive effects, beyond mere resource and skill transfer, which contribute to improving the global community and the environment.

There have been various concerns about the MNC activities, including the questions of the impact of MNC (Negandhi, 1980), civil societies' suspicion of MNCs as villains, (Yazji, 2006), or uneasy bedfellows in host countries (Prickett, 2003; Habib-Mintz, 2009). Despite the proven positive impacts that MNCs bring to the host country, such as job creation and technology transfer, the scope of corporate concerns has widened, ranging from labor issues, social equity, to the impact on the environment. The pressures have propelled MNCs to act more responsibly and render social benefits.

On the corporate side, addressing the issues of CSR became important as host governments and stakeholders began to raise higher standards of corporate activities. Therefore, compliance and generating social values became important activities for sustainable business in host countries (Negandhi, 1980; Sumantoro, 1984). Indeed, firm performance has become an amalgam of the inputs of a variety of stakeholder groups, including employees, shareholders, lenders, customers, suppliers, non-governmental organization (NGOs), and governments in global business (Dunning and Lundan, 2008a).

Thus, in order to reduce any tensions among different stakeholders of MNCs and to create more opportunities for both global community and the firm, we need new approaches such as CSV and CSO. The CSV was presented by Porter and Kramer (2011) as an extension to the studies of CSR to change the concept from compliance to value creation. Building on

---

[1] As the main investment policy trends, for example, the World Investment Report of the United Nations Conference on Trade and Development (UNCTAD, 2012) recognized the increasing need of sustainable development as part of the considerations in national and international investment policies, as well as in global frameworks such as the UN Guiding Principles on Business and Human Rights, the Principles for Responsible Agricultural Investment, the International Fund for Agricultural Development (IFAD) and the mandates from the Doha Conference, and the UN Conference on Sustainable Development Rio+20.

the CSV concept, CSO was presented in the works by Moon (2012a) and Moon, Parc, Yim, and Park (2011) to give strategic guidelines for CSV.

9.2. From Ethical Response to Creating Shared Value

The social activities of the firm trace back to Bowen's (1953) book titled, *Social Responsibilities of the Businessman*, which marked the beginning of the modern period of literature on CSR. Bowen argued that social responsibility is not a panacea, but it contains an important truth that must guide businesses in the future. With a significant attention paid to formalize and define CSR, Davis (1960) set forth the definition of social responsibility by arguing that it refers to businessmen's decisions and actions taken for reasons at least partially beyond the firm's direct economic or technical interest.

In the 1970s, the overall trajectory was towards an emphasis on how firms responded to social environments (Ackerman, 1973; Murray, 1976) and the effectiveness of social activities, i.e., corporate social performance (CSP). This is to move the field of "philanthropic duty" closer to the "business case" (Carroll, 1999; Sethi, 1975). Then there came Vogel (2005) who observed some features of the new world of CSR. He claimed that the new world of CSR is the link between CSR and corporate financial success. Studies seeking to link CSR to corporate financial performance (CFP) exploded during the 1980s, and the search for a tighter coupling with firm financial performance became popular (Lee, 2008).

This trend continued in the 1990s, and the quest for CSR accelerated in terms of its global outreach. The 1990s and 2000s became the era of global corporate citizenship (Frederick, 2008) which became preoccupied with the Enron Era of financial scandals (Carroll, 2009; Carroll and Shabana, 2010). The failure to recognize such interdependence in favor of putting business against society indeed led to reducing the productivity of CSR initiatives (Porter and Kramer, 2006). Thus, the focus of CSR theories was clearly shifting away, yet without any strategic directions, from an ethics-orientation to a performance-orientation.

In fact, corporate philanthropy is substantiated if it increases shareholder returns (Buchholtz, Amason, and Rutherford, 1999). Such trend of

CSR led to the emergence of competitive advantage justifications and value creation. Certain CSR activities allow firms to improve their competitiveness as stakeholder demands are seen as opportunities rather than constraints. Firms strategically manage their resources to meet these demands and exploit the opportunities associated with them for the benefit of the firm (Kurucz, Colbert, and Wheeler, 2008). In doing so, they avoid distractions from the core business, enhance the efficiency of their charitable activities, and assure unique value creation for the beneficiaries of the donor and the recipients.

This is because creating win–win outcomes between the donor and the recipient comes from satisfying stakeholders' demands and allowing the firm to pursue its business operations. As Drucker (1984) argued, "[t]he proper 'social responsibility' of business is to turn a social problem into economic opportunity and economic benefit, into productive capacity, into human competence, into well-paid jobs, and into wealth."

Thus, value-creation is about exploiting opportunities and reconciling the different stakeholder demands. When companies get "where and how" correctly, philanthropic activities and competitive advantage become mutually reinforcing and create a virtuous cycle (Porter and Kramer, 2002). When social activities are directed to the social issues where there is a convergence of interests between the economic gains and the social benefits, firms need to maximize the utility of the resources.

A more rigorous and active participation of private sector was seen possible with the concept of the bottom of the pyramid (BoP) markets. This theory, presented by Hart and Prahalad (2002), is one of the first studies to address the needs and the potential of the poor in the developing world. They emphasized that the bottom tier is the largest and represents the multi-trillion dollar market that holds a huge opportunity for business as well as technological innovation that can benefit both the company and the society.

Similarly, Bill Gates in his speech at the World Economic Forum in 2008 proposed a new approach for philanthropic activities, calling it "the creative capitalism" — an approach where governments, business, and nonprofits work together to stretch the reach of market forces. This is to allow more people to make a profit, gain recognition, and ease the world's inequities (Kinsley and Clarke, 2009).

The BoP strategy and the creative capitalism both redefine the role of business sector, especially in targeting the less privileged population in the world. Hart and Prahalad (2002) laid out foundations to setting strategies for effectively doing business in the BoP market, where Porter and Kramer (2011) provided a more in-depth strategic guidelines on corporate strategy in generating both social and economic values.

To formulate business strategies for social activities, Porter and Kramer (2011) introduced the terminology of CSV. They contended that firms must focus on what they are good at to increase the efficiency of social activities. If firms were to diverge their social activities from core businesses, they tend to increase opportunity costs coming from inefficient use of resources. This is different from CSR activities of giving one-time financial contribution. The CSV is to give social benefits to the recipients for them to be self-reliant in the future. In this way, the beneficiaries can in return become the sources of income for future businesses or co-developers of value creation. For example, Nestlé trained and provided farmers with better facilities and know-hows to produce quality milk for Nestlé's dairy products. By helping the farmers, Nestlé in return could produce better quality products for the market and reduce inefficiencies and problems relating to procurement.

9.3. CSO as International Business Strategies

The impact of CSV has been remarkable. CSV has been not only able to define where to target for social activities, but also to find the legitimacy to do so. It is no more about helping the others, but increasing efficiency for both the donor and the recipient. In doing so, the CSV connotes a procedural or prescriptive process of conducting strategic CSR. The CSV activities are summarized as three: 1) reconceiving products and markets, 2) redefining productivity in the value chain, and 3) enabling local cluster development (Porter and Kramer, 2011).

However, CSV in practice has still been understood as helping the recipients rather than on finding business opportunities and creating the self-reinforcing mechanism. Furthermore, CSV was not generically termed in contrast with CSR. This is why Moon (2012a) extended the concept in a generic matter with CSR and introduced the concept of CSO (see Figure 9.1).

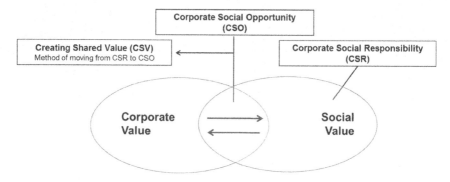

Figure 9.1   Comparing CSR, CSV, and CSO
Sources: Moon (2012a), and Moon et al. (2011).

CSO puts emphasis on how firms should not just focus on engaging in social activities to help the less privileged, but to co-create opportunities for both the society and the firm. The process of creating opportunities can be more efficiently done through collaborating with other parties. This is how firms can incorporate social activities to their core businesses to provide mutually beneficial outcomes. At the same time, firms can complement the disadvantages that may arise in their value chain activities. Thus, the CSO strategies for seeking competitiveness can be summarized as four essential steps (see Table 9.1).

Firstly, firms need to focus on their core competencies to increase the efficiency of social activities. Secondly, firms need to define social needs where they can complement their core activities the best. In many cases, the utility of the recipient may not match the intent of firm investment. In this regard, firms need to find the recipient segment that can benefit the most and, at the same time, contribute to the firm.

Thirdly, as firms do not always have enough resources, they often cannot address social and environmental issues alone. The effectiveness of social activities can be achieved through pooling resources and competencies together to exploit both economies of scope and scale. A portfolio of core competencies can be effective in finding synergistic impacts, than each firm's individual address of social issues which can create redundancies. Social and environmental problems we face are overwhelming for a single MNC to deal with. Social activities need to be dealt in cooperation with

Table 9.1. Four Strategies of CSO for Competitiveness

Four Strategies	Explanations
Focus on core competencies	• Find business related activities
	• Incorporate strategy
Help the related social segment	• Identify specific social needs
	• Design solutions through business factors
Overcome problems in the value chain	• Define any imbalances in value chain activities
	• Seek solutions from social factors
Collaborate with other organizations for better results	• Establish partnerships with other institutions
	• Maximize synergies or minimize costs

Note: Abstracted and extended from Moon (2012a).

other institutions and universities which can facilitate competence sharing. Lastly, through exchanges of skills, information, and other competencies, firms can take a broad look at their value chain activities and define any of its imbalances. As mentioned in Chapter 4 on the imbalance theory, addressing and fixing any imbalances can increase the overall competitiveness of firms. The good news is that they can solve firm imbalances by helping social problems and collaborating with other institutions.

9.4. Matching CSO with FDI Strategies

The four strategies to create CSO provide important implications for FDI strategies of the firm. With increasing social expectations of firms and heightened international regulations, MNCs constantly face new challenges to address in their operations. A failure to meet those pressures will tarnish the image and hurt the overall performance of businesses. The application of CSO, however, should not only be geared towards social activities of the firm in foreign locations, rather, it should be extended to seeking how firms can create values with the host country and maximize the benefits of FDI. This is to say, CSO strategies should provide guidelines in making sustainable investments in foreign locations as an extension to the ownership-location-internationalization (OLI) paradigm and to the imbalance theory (Yim, 2013).

In order to apply the four strategic steps of CSO to FDI, first of all, firms need to define both the core advantages that firms need to exploit and critical disadvantages in the value chain to address in host countries. This leads to the second step. FDI needs to take place to address any of the imbalances in its value chain activities. Complementing and enhancing the value chain activities should come from finding the mutual business opportunities in the host country.

Thus, when choosing a location, firms need to seek not only where they could complement their disadvantages, but also to solve host country's disadvantages. The reason that firms need to consider solving the problems of the host country goes back to our original idea that host countries are seeking benefits from MNC's presence (Yim, 2013). Without meeting the demands of the host country, social pressures may heighten on the investing firms and obstruct their long-term businesses in the host country. More than anything, the tangible benefits that MNCs bring to the host country can also shape host country's policies in favor of the investing firm, which can even bring "unexpected" benefits.

Furthermore, in order to continuously address changing resource challenges, MNCs need to spatially and virtually connect themselves with institutions, firms, and universities (see Chapter 6). Firm networks become the channel of resource and know-how exchanges, where particularly local firms, which have critical disadvantages, need to gain access to external resources that cannot be produced internally (Hite and Hesterly, 2001). They need to utilize these networks to access resources and capabilities, as they tend to lack necessary capital and legitimacy (e.g., Dubini and Aldrich, 1991). Thus, the collaboration builds up a mutually reliant and beneficial relationship that makes investment sustainable for both parties.

9.5. Beyond Sustainable FDI and CSO

As an extension to social activities of firms, let's take a look at how the development assistance given at the national level can help the developing countries. The development economics evolved after the two world wars as former colonial countries gained political independence, yet not the economic independence. During this period, scholars thought that developing countries cannot develop faster due to socio-economic structural problems stemming from rigidities in labor and land markets (Ohno and Ohno, 2002). After the 1970s, with a widening gap between the developed and developing countries (North-South problem), the developing countries blamed the developed countries for imposing unfair trade restrictions. MNCs were also blamed for taking advantage of the developing countries in the form of "neo-colonialism." Recognizing these issues, developed countries organized ODA as an instrument to help the developing countries and soothe the tensions created in the international arena.

Until recently, however, ODA that was given as loans or resources did not bring tangible economic development or poverty reduction in developing countries (Sunaga, 2004). The problem is that the process was often not clear in terms of how and where the donated resources were utilized in the recipient country. Even with transparent procedures, the resources were not utilized to their full extent and the actual benefit was not clear. Particularly, the resources were not transformed as a sustainable source for regional or economic development of the recipient country. Instead they remained no more than a short-term donation.

ODA, however, comes from tax payers' money in the donor country. The government, even for philanthropic purposes, should have responsibility to use taxpayers' money efficiently, especially if it were not to be served for domestic matters. Furthermore, along with the standards of the Millennium Development Goals and Paris Declaration set out by the international community, a need for aid effectiveness is compelling. In this regard, the direction of ODA is shifting from financial donations to a transfer of strategic policy guidelines where the government of the recipient country can implement cooperative framework involving stakeholders inside and outside the country (Ohno and Ohno, 2002). In order to make ODA more effective, the governments of donor countries are encouraged to partner with MNCs, along with civil society and non-governmental institutions and strive to co-create mutual benefits between the donor and the recipient countries.

In recent years, MNCs have been increasingly involved in ODA programs. If there are areas where MNCs can do a better job than the governments or public sectors, they are given initiative to utilize their expertise. If MNCs have skills to effectively tackle the needs of the recipient countries, the government had better partner with those firms. In doing so,

MNCs can also utilize their core competencies in the areas where they can create opportunities in their value chain activities. If MNCs, for example, are doing business in the location that has critical weakness in infrastructure obstructing their value chain activities, improving infrastructure creates mutual benefits both for the firm and the host country.

Often times, the area of donation is determined by the donor, from the donor's perspective, without rigorous analysis of the most needed area for the recipient. This is why despite their intent, donors make mistakes in spending the resources and efforts that do not complement the critical deficiency of the host country. In the end, they also lose motivations to sustain their support. Applying the concept of CSO, the donor can complement its deficiencies or enhance its core competitiveness by engaging in ODA. In the past, such investment has been criticized because interest-seeking assistance was not acceptable under the context of philanthropy. However, if MNCs need motivation to continue their assistance to the development of society, they have to benefit from social activities.

Here again, collaboration among firms and other institutions is effective. For example, establishing and upgrading infrastructure is a massive work, so a single donor country or a firm may not be able to effectively solve the problem. A group of firms with different expertise in building various fields of infrastructure should thus come together and take responsibility of their own expertise. This consortium type of collaboration will reduce redundancy and inefficiency of contributions of donors (see Figure 9.2). It does not matter whether the donor is a public or private sector. What is important is to let each firm or institution do its role to help the social project, and at the same time enhance its competitiveness. Firm's social activities should involve more business mindset than just philanthropic intent.

9.6. Towards an Integrated Framework for Global Development Strategy

9.6.1. *Industrial Eco-City Development (IECD): Hardware*

In the long run, the most important contribution to the host country for its self-sufficiency is to help develop skills and entrepreneurship through training workers and transferring management techniques. The living and working conditions are also important for gaining the needed skills.

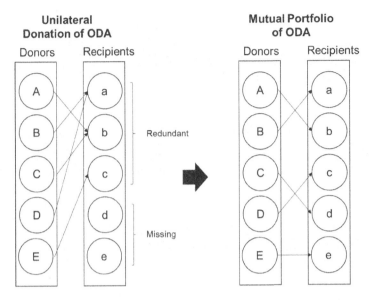

Figure 9.2 Effective Portfolio for Sustainable ODA Strategies
Note: This Figure was revised from Moon's (2012a) CSR activities to explain ODA.

However, when MNCs establish manufacturing facilities to exploit cheap labor in developing countries, they tend to build industrial factories in a remote area that is disconnected from the city. Local workers are only provided with small dorm rooms and they are provided with few after-work leisure activities. Such reality of MNCs' investment demotivates young workers to continue working. They leave the company to move to the city, or to work for another company and seek a better life.

Yet, such minimum level of investments on workers in the developing countries does not minimize the costs of the entire business operations. The high turnover rate of workers in fact costs the MNCs more than providing a favorable working conditions as they have to recruit new workers and train them. This also makes it hard for firms to upgrade workers' skills. Therefore, this will leave the manufacturing facility as a low-skilled workplace and fail to attract high-skilled workers.

With a rapid development of economies and information technology, the young workers in developing countries no longer merely seek monetary compensation. They demand similar leisure activities and lifestyle as the young people in more developed countries do. A good working condition and favorable living environment can be developed in three stages as follows.

For a favorable industrial complex, MNCs first need to develop a core company in a host country, and transfer specific sets of skills and entrepreneurial capabilities, so it can attract good workers. Building the skills of local workers will give a positive effect on the host country. Trained workers can work for the company, work in other companies, or start up new local companies. Any of these alternatives will create knowledge spillover and increase the employment of the host country. In the second stage, MNCs can create backward and forward linkages with local firms or other foreign firms to build local firms' competitiveness. Such linkages stimulate local suppliers and enhance local competition, which will be the driving force for further development. In the final stage, firms can build a web of firm clusters that can promote a vigorous transfer of knowledge and skills. A good example is Bangalore in India, where firms have formed a cluster and are linked to Silicon Valley in the US (see Chapter 6). The global linkage of clusters between the developed and developing countries will then further facilitate to exchange and create knowledge.

For a favorable living environment, housing and infrastructure (telecommunication and transportation systems) as well as schools and hospitals can attract local workers to agglomerate around the industrial complex. However, the next stage has to go beyond just being the biologically "living" environment; the locations have to be culturally "livable". There is a need for entertainment-and-leisure complexes that can satisfy and promote after-work life. This in return motivates workers to work better and provides another incentive to continue their career path in that specific company or region. The final stage is to build a city through agglomeration effects with a portfolio of various sets of functions that can transform the region to a "city." A good example is Singapore's Fusionopolis, a complex of the newest mega-science facilities to spur inter-disciplinary research with the world's best housing facilities and entertainment centers. The motto of the city is to "work, live, and play" (A*Star, 2009).

9.6.2. *Industrial Eco-City Development (IECD): Software*

In development studies, national economic growth is usually perceived to take similar paths but only at a different pace (e.g., Inglehart, 1997). If countries reach a certain level of development (i.e., through technological or institutional development), they will be facilitated to develop further.

Industry structure may change similarly, from low-tech to high-tech industries, and from labor-intensive industries to knowledge-intensive industries, but the reason that they change differently at a different pace is determined by their socio-cultural aspects. This means that along with the development of "hardware" (industrial and living complex), there is a need for the "software" (mechanism) that can trigger the country to absorb and learn to develop.

The socio-cultural aspect is highly associated with the host country's motivation and strategy. As for the motivation, a social motivation campaign may have a big influence throughout the nation to educate local workers and enhance their absorptive capacities (Minbaeva *et al.*, 2003). For example, a national campaign called the New Village Movement (*Saemaul Undong*) was initiated under President Park Chung-hee's regime in the 1970s to promote the rapid development of Korean agricultural and industrial sectors. This campaign was initiated to increase the agricultural productions to meet the increasing domestic demands. It later became one of the most effective national movements for regional (rural) development. Such campaign became the foundation to a strong public motivation for self-help, hard work, and cooperation to achieve industrial development within a short period of time.

The socio-cultural software can also be transferred to other countries. This can be seen in the case of Japanese one-village-one-product (OVOP). This was the policy of the Japanese from the late 1970s to promote regional development by focusing on the areas in which each village had competitive advantage. They targeted to develop the best product from each village. When OVOP was exported to Thailand, it was changed to one-Tambon-one-product (OTOP).[2] The purpose was to revive the local firms that may have potential to develop further. The selected enterprises make the products and export to foreign markets by upgrading their current product lines. However, there still needs further improvement in localizing the Japanese strategies for practical applications (see Chapter 1). In terms of sustainability and effectiveness, OTOP has not yet brought tangible success, and this calls for a global development satrategy.

For software ODA, the most efficient methods of firm and national capabilities that promote rapid catch-up of economic development need

---

[2] Tambon stands for "village" in Thailand.

to be set. The methods share the commonalities of agility, benchmarking, convergence, and dedication (see Chapter 4). First, the donor countries need to precisely deliver the needs in a timely manner. The issue lies not only in the effectiveness, but how rapidly the recipients are experiencing the development.

Second, the donors need to share and emulate the best practices done in other countries. Currently international organizations and non-governmental institutions have set platforms for countries to benchmark and learn from each other's experiences in enhancing aid effectiveness and raising public awareness (OECD, 2009). In doing so, donor countries form development cooperation among themselves to more effectively tackle the problem through exchanging experiences. The Northern contributors (or the developed countries), with a larger amount of financial support and higher skill-sets, are partnering with the South. This is called as the Triangular development cooperation (North–South–South cooperation), mixing experiences from the countries that are still developing as they are often in a better position to respond and deal with the needs in the countries of aid recipients.

The emphasis on sharing the developing countries' experience is well illustrated in the triangular relationship formed between India, Brazil, and South Africa. By sharing similar challenges that they face, they are promoting exchanges and strengthening capacity in agriculture, education, culture, and science and technology together (Soule-Kohndou, 2013; OECD, 2009). Such process of convergence across countries and regions has led to the creation of mechanism of peer scrutiny and ultimately to a greater efficiency.

Lastly, the major lessons learned from ODA experiences were largely concerned with a lack of coherence in strategies, policies, and governance system. The 2009 Development Assistance Committee (DAC) Peer Reviews summarized that countries need to have a clear, top level statement of the purpose that has wide ownership and can remain relevant for a sufficient period of time, to set a clear mandate and establish mechanism for aid effectiveness, and to promote coherence between diverse aspects of multilateral aid. They also stated that for aid effectiveness, "securing and developing well-qualified, motivated local and expatriate staff is essential" (OECD, 2009). In this sense, a strong dedication of ODA programs, with a clear motivation and goal sets, enables donor countries to make greater

Table 9.2.   Four Steps to Smart ODA

Four Steps		Explanations
CSR-type of ODA	Compliance	A minimum level of compliance of international standards to avoid international criticisms and pressure
	Self-satisfaction	Philanthropic donation of the donor country without much aid effectiveness for the recipient
CSO-type of ODA	Image	Trust and favorable image and a good relationship-building
	Competitiveness	Strategic ODA programs to enhance both the competitiveness of the donor and the recipient

Note: This table was adapted and extended from Moon's (2012a) CSR table to explain ODA types.

strides for their shared goal (OECD, 2009) and at the same time increase the competitiveness of the donor and the recipient countries.

However, the ODA activity has in practice, remained at a philanthropic level (CSR-type)(see Table 9.2). This means that donor countries are striving merely to meet global standards that are imposed upon them (i.e., increasing the ODA amount compared to their gross domestic product). They also engage in ODA programs without much assessment done in the recipient countries. In this sense, they are lacking in strategy-building and effective evaluation. Therefore, donor countries should strive for CSO-type of ODA, seeking sustainability, rather than just CSR-type of ODA. Through well-designed ODA grants they enhance their image and reputation in the recipient countries and in the international community. This will strengthen the donor-recipient relationships and will mitigate or even reverse developing countries' dependency theory. The donor and the recipient countries should move from being merely "good" to seeking "smart" strategies, building mechanisms for mutual value creation.

As the role of MNCs has expanded to non-business sectors such as in ODA, the CSO concept should be the key to creating mutual values in global economy. Particularly with increasingly interdependent relationships between MNCs and local society, the role of national government to foster an integrated global business environment has become more important than ever. In this context, ODA has also become an important area which calls for an active role of MNCs.

As a coordinator of ODA strategy, national governments need to consider how and where firms should make investments (hardware ODA) and what mechanisms developing countries should build for a self-reliant economy (software ODA). The construction of both hardware (industrial and living environment) and software (motivation and strategy), from just an industrial cluster to an eco-city called IECD can be a foundation to the most efficient development strategies with which MNCs and national government can collaborate.

9.7. Conclusion

Firms are increasingly faced with heightened social pressure and international regulations to "give back" to the global society as a global citizen. However, such philanthropic approach has indeed created large inefficiencies in resource allocation. Philanthropic social activities are not sustainable and can be in fact regarded as another kind of "expenses" to firms. Thus, in order to enhance the resource efficiency and sustain the effectiveness by creating new business opportunities, this chapter introduced Moon's (2012a) concept of CSO, which is extended from Porter and Kramer's (2011) CSV concept. The CSO concept holds a great significance for MNCs in rapidly changing environments as it gives guidelines in sustaining their investments in host countries. This concept also incorporates both the OLI paradigm and the imbalance theory in a sense that firms need to utilize their ownership advantages to transform any costs and disadvantages of doing business in foreign locations into new business opportunities.

In finalizing the book, this chapter takes one step further to give strategic framework for ODA programs where MNCs have increasingly played an important role towards building shared objectives and development efforts in creating a self-reliant economy of the recipient countries. The application of the CSO concept in international realm gives meaningful implications for global managers and national policy makers, to co-create shared values for both the MNCs and host countries.

References

Ackerman, R.W. (1973). How Companies Respond to Social Demands, *Harvard Business Review*, 51(4): 88–98.

Adams, S. (2012). Apple's New Foxconn Embarrassment, *Forbes*, December 9, 2012.

Adler, P.S. and Kwon, S.W. (2002). Social Capital: Prospects for a New Concept, *Academy of Management Review*, 27(1): 17–40.

Aitken, B.J. and Harrison, A.E. (1999). Do Domestic Firms Benefit from Direct Foreign Investment? Evidence from Venezuela, *American Economic Review*, 89(3): 605–618.

Alabama Development Office. Available at http://www.choosealabama.net/index.php/alabama-development-office.

Amin, A. (1994). The Difficult Transition from Informal Economy to Marshallian Industrial Districts, *Area*, 26(1): 13–24.

Amsden, A.H. (2001). *The Rise of the Rest: Challenges to the West from Late-Industrializing Economies*, New York: Oxford University Press.

Amsden, A.H. and Hikino, T. (1994). Project Execution Capability, Organizational Know-how and Conglomerate Corporate Growth in Late Industrialization, *Industrial and Corporate Change*, 3(1): 111–147.

Anderson, E. and Gatignon, H. (1986). Modes of Foreign Entry: A Transaction Cost Analysis and Propositions, *Journal of International Business Studies*, 17: 1–26.

Andriopoulos, C. and Lewis, M.W. (2009). Exploitation–Exploration Tensions and Organizational Ambidexterity: Managing Paradoxes of Innovation, *Organization Science*, 20(4): 696–717.

Arrow, K. (1974). *The Limits of Organization*, New York: W.W. Norton.

Asia-Pacific Research Center (2003). *Center Overview 2003*, Stanford University. Available at http://iis-db.stanford.edu/pubs/20426/APARC_Overview_2003.pdf.

Agency for Science and Technology and Research (A*Star) (2009). *A*Star Homepage*. Available at http://www.a-star.edu.sg/Biopolis-Fusionopolis/A-Great-Place-to-Work-Live-Play/One-North.aspx.

Bain, J.S. (1956). *Barriers to New Competition: Their Character and Consequences in Manufacturing Industries*, Cambridge: Harvard University Press.

Baker, S. (1991). The Mexico Pact: Worth the Price, *Business Week*, May 26: 32–35.

Barney, J.B. (1991). Firm Resources and Sustained Competitive Advantage, *Journal of Management*, 17(1): 99–120.

Bartlett, C.A. (1986). Building and Managing the Transnational: The New Organizational Challenge. In Porter, M.E. (ed.), *Competition in Global Industries*, Boston: Harvard Business School.

Bartlett, C.A. and Ghoshal, S. (1989). *Managing Across Borders: The Multinational Solution*, London: Harvard Business School Press.

Bartlett, C.A. and Ghoshal, S. (1999). *Managing Across Borders: The Transnational Solution*, 2nd Edition, Cambridge: Harvard Business School Press.

Beamish, P.W. and Banks, J.C. (1987). Equity Joint Ventures and the Theory of the Multinational Enterprise, *Journal of International Business Studies*, 18(2): 10–16.

Benito, G.R.G. and Gripsrud, G. (1992). The Expansion of Foreign Direct Investments: Discrete Rational Location Choices or a Cultural Learning Process, *Journal of International Business Studies*, 23(3): 461–476.

Bevan, A.A. and Estrin, S. (2000). The Determinants of Foreign Direct Investment in Transition Economies, William Davidson Institute, Working Paper No. 342.

Bilkey, W.J. and Nes, E. (1982). Country-of-Origin Effects on Product Evaluations, *Journal of International Business Studies*, 13(1): 89–99.

Blomström, M. and Kokko, A. (1997). Foreign Direct Investment and Politics: The Swedish Model. In Dunning, J.H. (ed.), *Globalization, Governments and Competitiveness*, Oxford: Oxford University Press.

Bowen, H.R. (1953). *Social Responsibilities of the Businessman*, New York: Harper & Row.

Boyacigiller, N., Kleinberg, M.J., Phillips, M.E. and Sackmann, S. (1996). Conceptualizing Culture. In Punnet, B.J. and Shenkar, O. (eds.), *Handbook for International Management Research*, Cambridge: Blackwell.

Branstetter, L.G. and Feenstra, R.C. (2002). Trade and Foreign Direct Investment in China: A Political Economy Approach, *Journal of International Economics*, 58(2): 335–358.

Brewer, P.A. (2007). Operationalizing Psychic Distance: A Revised Approach, *Journal of International Marketing*, 15(1): 44–66.

Buckley, P.J. and Casson, M. (1976). *The Future of the Multinational Enterprise*, London: MacMillan Press.

Buckley, P.J. and Casson, M. (1981). The Optimal Timing of a Foreign Direct Investment, *The Economic Journal*, 91(361): 75–87.

Bunker, S. and Ciccantell, P.S. (2007). *East Asia and the Global Economy: Japan's Ascent, with Implications for China's Future*, Baltimore, MD: Johns Hopkins University Press.

Calof, J.L. (1993). The Mode Choice and Change Decision Process and Its Impact on International Performance, *International Business Review*, 2(1): 97–120.

Calvet, A.L. (1981). A Synthesis of Foreign Direct Investment Theories and Theories of Multinational Firm, *Journal of International Business Studies*, 12: 43–59.

Camagni, R. (2002). On the Concept of Territorial Competitiveness: Sound or Misleading? *Urban Studies*, 39(13): 2395–2411.

Carroll, A.B. (1999). Corporate Social Responsibility: Evolution of a Definitional Construct, *Business and Society*, 38: 268–295.

Carroll, A.B. (2009). A Look at the Future of Business Ethics, *Athens Banner-Herald*, January 10.

Carroll, A.B. and Shabana, K.M. (2010). The Business Case for Corporate Social Responsibility: A Review of Concepts, Research and Practice, *International Journal of Management Reviews*, 12(1): 85–105.

Caves, R.E. (1974). Multinational Firms, Competition, and Productivity in Host-Country Markets, *Economica*, 41(162): 176–193.

Chandler, A.D. (1990). *Strategy and Structure: Chapters in the History of the Industrial Enterprise*, Cambridge: MIT Press.

Chen, E.K.Y. and Lin, P. (2005). *Outward Foreign Direct Investment from Hong Kong*, Hong Kong: Lingnan University.

Chesbrough, H. (1999). The Organizational Impact of Technological Change: A Comparative Theory of National Institutional Factors, *Industrial and Corporate Change*, 8: 447–485.

Chi, T. (1994). Trading in Strategic Resources: Necessary Conditions, Transaction Cost Problems, and Choice of Exchange Structure, *Strategic Management Journal*, 15: 271–290.

Cho, D.S. (1994). A Dynamic Approach to International Competitiveness: The Case of Korea, *Journal of Far Eastern Business*, 1(1): 17–36.

Cho, D.S. and Moon, H.C. (2013a). *From Adam Smith to Michael Porter: Evolution of Competitive Theory*, (Extended Edition), Singapore: World Scientific Publishing, Co. Pte. Ltd.

Cho, D.S. and Moon, H.C. (2013b). *International Review of National Competitiveness: A Detailed Analysis of Sources and Rankings*, Cheltenham: Edward Elgar.

Clapp, D. (2002). Success Stories: Teamwork Drives Hyundai to Alabama! *Business Facilities*, August, 2002.

CNNMoney (2012). *Apple's $46 Billion Sales Set New Tech Record*. Available at http://money.cnn.com/2012/01/24/technology/apple_earnings/index.htm.

Coase, R.H. (1937). The Nature of the Firm, *Economica*, 4: 386–405. Reprinted in Williamson, O.E. and Winter, S. (eds.) (1991), *The Nature of the Firm: Origins, Evolution, and Development*, New York: Oxford University Press.

Cohen, W.M. and Levinthal, D.A. (1990). Absorptive Capacity: A New Perspective on Learning and Innovation, *Administrative Science Quarterly*, 35: 128–152.

Colombo, M.G. (1998). *The Changing Boundaries of the Firm: Explaining Evolving Inter-Firm Relations*, New York: Routledge.

Cox, T.H. and Blake, S. (1991). Managing Cultural Diversity: Implications for Organizational Competitiveness, *The Executive*, 5(3): 45–56.

Cuervo-Cazurra, A. and Genc, M. (2008). Transforming Disadvantages into Advantages: Developing-Country MNCs in the Least Developed Countries, *Journal of International Business Studies*, 39: 957–979.

Cushman, D.O. (1985). Real Exchange Rate Risk, Expectations and the Level of Direct Investment, *Review of Economics and Statistics*, 67: 297–308.

Davis, K. (1960). Can Business Afford to Ignore Social Responsibilities? *California Management Review*, 2(Spring): 70–76.

D'Costa, A.P. (2004) Export Growth and Path Dependence: The Locking-in of Innovations in the Software Industry. In D'Costa, A.P. and Sridharan, E. (eds.), *India in the Global Software Industry: Innovation, Firm Strategies and Development*, New Delhi: Palgrave Macmillan.

D'Costa, A.P. (2011). Geography, Uneven Development and Distributive Justice: The Political Economy of IT Growth in India, *Cambridge Journal of Regions, Economy and Society*, 4(2): 237–251.

Devinney T.M., Midgley, D.F. and Venaik, S. (2000). Optimal Performance of the Global Firm: Formalizing and Extending the Integration-Responsiveness Framework, *Organization Science*, 11(6): 674–695.

Dixit, A. and Norman, V. (1980). *Theory of International Trade: A Dual, General Equilibrium Approach*, Cambridge: Cambridge University Press.

Drucker, P.F. (1984). The New Meaning of Corporate Social Responsibility, *California Management Review*, 26: 53–63.

Dubini, P and Aldrich, H. (1991). Personal and Extended Networks are Central to the Entrepreneurial Process, *Journal of Business Venturing*, 6(5): 305–313.

Dunning, J.H. (1958). *American Investment in British Manufacturing Industry*, London: Allen & Unwin. Reprinted in Dunning, J.H. (1976), *American Investment in British Manufacturing Industry*, New York: Arno Press.

Dunning, J.H. (1980). Toward an Eclectic Theory of International Production: Some Empirical Tests, *Journal of International Business Studies*, 11(1): 9–31.

Dunning, J.H. (1993). *Multinational Enterprises and the Global Economy*, Wokingham and Reading: Addison Wesley.

Dunning, J.H. (1997). *Alliance Capitalism and Global Business*, London: Routledge.

Dunning, J.H. (1998). Location and the Multinational Enterprise: A Neglected Factor, *Journal of International Business Studies*, 29(1): 45–66.

Dunning, J.H. (2000). The Eclectic Paradigm as an Envelope for Economic and Business Theories of MNC Activity, *International Business Review*, 9: 163–190.

Dunning, J.H (2001a). The OLI Paradigm of International Production: Past, Present and Future, *International Journal of the Economics of Business*, 8(2): 173–190.

Dunning, J.H. (2001b). Explaining Changing Patterns of International Production: In Defense of the Eclectic Theory, *International Journal of the Economics of Business*, 8(2): 173–190.

Dunning, J.H. Fujita, M. and Yakova, N. (2007). Some Macro-data on the Region-alization/Globalization Debate: A Comment on the Rugman/Verbeke Analysis, *Journal of International Business Studies*, 38: 177–199.

Dunning, J.H. and Rugman, A.M (1985). The Influence of Hymer's Dissertation on the Theory of Foreign Direct Investment, *The American Economic Review*, 75(2): 228–232.

Dunning, J.H. and Lundan, S.M. (2008a). *Multinational Enterprises and the Global Economy*, Cheltenham and Northampton: Edward Elgar Publishing.

Dunning, J.H. and Lundan, S.M. (2008b). Institutions and the OLI Paradigm of the Multinational Enterprise, *Asia Pacific Journal of Management*, 25: 573–593.

Dyer, J.H. and Singh, H. (1998). The Relational View: Cooperative Strategy and Sources of Inter-organizational Competitive Advantage, *Academy of Management Journal*, 23(4): 660–679.

Economist. (2000). Foreign Friends, *The Economist*, January 8, 2000.

Economist (2010). Japanese Firms in China, Culture Shock: Chinese Labour Unrest is Forcing Japanese Bosses to Change, *The Economist*, July 8, 2010.

European Commission (2002). *Regional Clusters in Europe: Observatory of European SMEs*, 3. Available at http://ec.europa.eu/regional_policy/archive/innovation/pdf/library/regional_clusters.pdf.

Eisenhardt, K.M. and Martin, J.A. (2000). Dynamic Capabilities: What Are They? *Strategic Management Journal*, 21: 1105–1121.

Farrell, D. (2004). Beyond Offshoring: Assess Your Company's Global Potential, *Harvard Business Review*, 82(12): 82–90.

Feinberg, S.E. and Majumdar, S.K. (2001). Technology Spillovers from Foreign Direct Investment in the Indian Pharmaceutical Industry, *Journal of International Business Studies*, 32: 421–437.

Florida, R. and Kenney, M. (1994). Institutions and Economic Transformation: The Case of Postwar Japanese Capitalism, *Growth and Change*, 25(2): 247–262.

Fontagné, L. (1999). *Foreign Direct Investment and International Trade: Complements or Substitutes?* OECD Science, Technology and Industry Working Papers: OECD Publishing.

Franco, C., Rentocchini, F., and Marzetti, G.V. (2008). Why Do Firms Invest Abroad? An Analysis of the Motives Underlying Foreign Direct Investments, *The IUP Journal of International Business Law*, 9 (1&2): 42–65.

Frederick, W.C. (2008). Corporate Social Responsibility: Deep Roots, Flourishing Growth, Promising Future. In Crane, A., McWilliams, A., Matten, D., Moon, J. and Siegel, D. (eds.), *The Oxford Handbook of Corporate Social Responsibility*, Oxford: Oxford University Press.

Gabbay, S.M. and Zuckerman, E.W. (1998). Social Capital and Opportunity in Corporate R&D: The Contingent Effect of Contact Density and Mobility Expectations, *Social Science Research*, 27: 189–217.

Gencay, R. and Stengos, T. (1998). Moving Average Rules, Volume and the Predictability of Security Returns with Feedforward Networks, *Journal of Forecasting*, 17: 401–414.

Gerlach, M.L. (1992). *Alliance Capitalism: The Social Organization of Japanese Business*, Berkeley: University of California Press.

Ghemawat, P. and Khanna, T. (1998). The Nature of Diversified Business Groups: A Research Design and Two Case Studies, *Journal of Industrial Economics*, 46(1): 35–61.

Goetz, M. and Niedzialkowskiego, U. (2008). Cluster, Competitiveness, Attractiveness, Innovativeness — How Do They Fit Together? *Proceedings of the 5th International Conference on Innovation & Management*, 10–11 December, UNU-MERIT, Maastricht, The Netherlands. Available at http://www.pucsp.br/icim/ingles/proceedings/proceedings_2008.html.

Grossman, G.M. and Helpman, E. (1994). Endogenous Innovation in the Theory of Growth, *Journal of Economic Perspectives*, 8(1): 23–44.

Guillen, M. F. (2000). Business Groups in Emerging Economies: A Resource-Based View, *Academy of Management Journal*, 43(3): 362–380.

Guillen, M.F. and Garcia-Canal, E. (2009). The American Model of the Multinational Firm and the "New" Multinationals from Emerging Economies, *Academy of Management Perspectives*, 23(2): 23–35.

Gulati, R. (1998). Alliances and Networks, *Strategic Management Journal*, 19(4): 293–317.

Ha, B.K. (2003). *The Post-Industrialization Process of Korean Economy: The Effects of Foreign Direct Investment*, Report prepared for Industry Research Seminar (in Korean).

Habib-Mintz, N. (2009). Multinational Corporations' Role in Improving Labour Standards in Developing Countries, *Journal of International Business and Economy*, 10(2): 39–58.

Han, M. and Terpstra, V. (1988). Country-of-Origin Effects for Uni-National and Bi-National Products, *Journal of International Business Studies*, 19(2): 235–255.

Harris, P. (2012). Apple Hit by Boycott Call over Worker Abuses in China, *The Guardian*, January 29, 2012.

Harrison, A. and McMillan, M. (2011). Offshoring Jobs? Multinationals and US Manufacturing Employment, *Review of Economics and Statistics*, 93(3): 857–875.

Hart, S. and Prahalad, C.K. (2002). The Fortune at the Bottom of the Pyramid, *Strategy+Business*, 26: 54–67.

Harzing, A.W. (2002). Acquisitions versus Greenfield Investments: International Strategy and Management of Entry Modes, *Strategic Management Journal*, 23: 211–227.

He, Z.L. and Wong, P.K. (2004). Exploration vs. Exploitation: An Empirical Test of the Ambidexterity Hypothesis, *Organization Science*, 15(4): 481–494.

Helpman, E. (1981). International Trade in the Presence of Product Differentiation, Economies of Scale and Monopolistic Competition: A Chamberlin–Heckscher–Ohlin Approach, *Journal of International Economics*, 11(3): 305–340.

Hennart, J.F. (1982). *A Theory of Multinational Enterprise*, Ann Arbor: University of Michigan.

Hill, C.W. (2013). *International Business: Competing in the Global Marketplace*, New York: McGraw-Hill Irwin.

Hill, C.W., Hwang, P. and Kim, W.C. (1990). An Eclectic Theory of the Choice of International Entry Mode, *Strategic Management Journal*, 11: 117–128.

Hill, C.W.L., Wee, C. and Udayasanker, K. (2012). *International Business: An Asian Perspective*, Singapore: Mc-Graw Hill Education.

Hite, J.M. and Hesterly, W.S. (2001). The Evolution of Firm Networks: From Emergence to Early Growth of the Firm, *Strategic Management Journal*, 22: 275–286.

HMMA. (2014). *Hyundai Motors Manufacturing Alabama website*. Available at http://www.hmmausa.com/?page_id=79.

Hobday, M. (1995). *Innovation in East Asia: The Challenge of Japan*, Cheltenham: Edward Elgar.

Hofstede, G. (1980). *Culture's Consequences: International Differences in Work-Related Values*, Beverly Hills: Sage.

Hofstede, G. (1983). The Cultural Relativity of Organizational Practices and Theories, *Journal of International Business Studies*, 14(2): 75–89.

Hofstede, G. (1991). *Cultures and Organizations: Software of the Mind*, New York: McGraw-Hill.

Hofstede, G. (2007). Asian Management in the 21st Century, *Asia Pacific Journal of Management*, 24(4): 411–420.

Hofstede, G., Hofstede, G.J. and Minkov, M. (2010). *Cultures and Organizations: Software of the Mind* (Rev. 3rd Edition), New York: McGraw-Hill.

Hood, N. and Young, S. (1979). *The Economics of Multinational Enterprise*, London: Longman.

Horaguchi, H. and Toyne, B. (1990). Setting the Record Straight: Hymer, Internalization Theory and Transaction Cost Economics, *Journal of International Business Studies*, 21(3): 487–494.

Hwa, N.E. (2007). *Different Uses of Moving Average (MA)*. Available at http://www.chartnexus. com/learning/static/pulses_apr2007.pdf.

Hymer, S. (1976[1960]). *The International Operations of National Firms: A Study of Foreign Direct Investment*, Cambridge: MIT Press.

Inglehart, R. (1997). Modernization and Postmodernization: Cultural, Economic, and Political Change in 43 Societies, *Canadian Journal of Political Science*, 31(2): 391–392.

International Institute for Management Development (IMD) (2013). *IMD World Competitiveness Yearbook* 2013, Geneva: IMD.

Itoh, M. and Kiyono, K. (1988). Foreign Trade and Direct Investment, *Industrial Policy of Japan*, 155–182.

Jack. A. (1997). French Go into Overdrive to Win Investment, *Financial Times*, December 10, 1997.

Kindleberger, C.P. (1969). *American Business Abroad*, New Haven: Yale University Press.

Kinsley, M. and Clarke, C. (2009). *Creative Capitalism: A Conversation with Bill Gates, Warren Buffett, and Other Economic Leaders*, Great Britain: Simon & Schuster.

Knickerbocker, F.T. (1973). Oligopolistic Reaction and Multinational Enterprise, *The International Executive*, 15(2): 7–9.

Kogut, B. and Zander, U. (1992). Knowledge of the Firm, Combinative Capabilities, and the Replication of Technology, *Organization Science*, 3(3): 383–397.

Kogut, B. and Zander, U. (2003). Knowledge of the Firm and the Evolutionary Theory of the Multinational Corporation, *Journal of International Business Studies*, 34: 516–529.

Koruna, S. (2004). Leveraging Knowledge Assets: Combinative Capabilities-Theory and Practice, *R&D Management*, 34(5): 505–516.

Kraatz, M.S. (1998). Learning by Association? Inter-organizational Networks and Adaptation to Environmental Change, *Academy of Management Journal*, 41: 621–643.

Krugman, P. (1979). Increasing Returns, Monopolistic Competition and International Trade, *Journal of International Economics*, 9(4): 469–479.

Krugman, P. (1980). Scale Economies, Product Differentiation, and the Pattern of Trade, *American Economic Review*, 70(5): 950–959.

Krugman, P. (1991a). *Geography and Trade*, Cambridge: The MIT Press.

Krugman, P. (1991b). Increasing Returns and Economic Geography, *Journal of Political Economy*, 99(3): 483–499.

Kurucz, E., Colbert, B. and Wheeler, D. (2008). The Business Case for Corporate Social Responsibility. In Crane, A., McWilliams, A., Matten, D., Moon, J. and Siegel, D. (eds.), *The Oxford Handbook of Corporate Social Responsibility*, Oxford: Oxford University Press.

Lecraw, D.J. (1993). Outward Direct Investment by Indonesian firms: Motivation and Effects, *Journal of International Business Studies*, 24(3): 589–600.

Lee, M.P. (2008). A Review of the Theories of Corporate Social Responsibility: Its Evolutionary Path and the Road Ahead, *International Journal of Management Reviews*, 10: 53–73.

Lee, W.B. and Kwon, Y.C. (2006). Global Firm's Dynamic Capability and Strategic Alliance: A Case of Samsung Electronics, *Korean Business Education Research*, 9(2): 63–86 (in Korean).

Leonard-Barton, D. (1992). Core Capabilities and Core Rigidities: A Paradox in Managing New Product Development, *Strategic Management Journal*, 13(S1): 111–125.

Li, J.J. (2005). The Formation of Managerial Networks of Foreign Firms in China: The Effects of Strategic Orientation, *Asia Pacific Journal of Management*, 22(4): 423–443.

Li, X. and Liu, X. (2005). Foreign Direct Investment and Economic Growth: An Increasingly Endogenous Relationship, *World Development*, 33(3): 393–407.

Lieberman, M.B. and Montgomery, D.B. (1988). First-Mover Advantages, *Strategic Management Journal*, 9(S1): 41–58.

Lieberman, M.B. and Montgomery, D.B. (1998). First-Mover (Dis)Advantages: Retrospective and Link with the Resource-Based View, *Strategic Management Journal*, 19: 1111–1125.

Lipsey, R.E. (1995). Outward Direct Investment and the US Economy, In Feldstein, M., Hines, J.R. Jr. and Hubbard, R.G. (eds.), *The Effects of Taxation on Multinational Corporations*, London: University Of Chicago Press.

Lipsey, R.E. (2000). Inward FDI and Economic Growth in Developing Countries, *Transnational Corporations*, 9(1): 67–96.

Lipsey, R.E. (2002). Foreign Production by US Firms and Parent Firm Employment, In Lipsey, R.E. and Mucchielli, J. (eds.), *Multinational Firms and Impacts on Employment, Trade and Technology: New Perspectives for a New Century*. London: Routledge.

Lipsey, R.E. (2004). Home-and Host-Country Effects of Foreign Direct Investment, In Baldwin, R.E. and Winters, L.A. (ed.), *Challenges to Globalization: Analyzing the Economics*, Chicago: University of Chicago Press.

Lipsey, R.E. and Sjöholm, F. (2005). *The Impact of Inward FDI on Host Countries: Why Such Different Answers?* Washington DC: Institute for International Economics and Center for Global Development, 23–43.

Loesch, A. (Woglom W.H., Trans.) (1954). *The Economics of Location*, New Haven: Yale University Press.

March, J.G. (1991). Exploration and Exploitation in Organizational Learning, *Organization Science*, 2(1): 71–67.

Marshall, A. (1920[1890]). *Principle of Economics*, London, Macmillan.

Martin, R. and Sunley, P. (2003). Deconstructing Clusters: Chaotic Concept or Policy Panacea? *Journal of Economic Geography*, 3(1): 5–35.

Meng, B. and Miroudot, S. (2011). Towards Measuring Trade in Value Added and Other Indicators of Global Value Chains: Current OECD Work Using I/O Tables, Presented at the *Global Forum on Trade Statistics*, Geneva: Eurostat, UNSD and WTO.

Minbaeva, D., Pedersen, T., Björkman, I., Fey, C. F. and Park, H.J. (2003). MNC Knowledge Transfer, Subsidiary Absorptive Capacity, and HRM, *Journal of International Business Studies*, 34(6): 586–599.

Minister of Commerce Industry and Energy (MCIE) (2003). *Status of Outward Foreign Direct Investment in Manufacturing and Analysis of the Survey Results*. Available at http://www.kdi.re.kr/infor/ep_view.jsp?num=66513.

Modén, K.M. (1998). Foreign Acquisitions of Swedish Companies: Effects on R&D and Productivity, *ISA Studies*, 1998(2), Stockholm: Research Institute of Industrial Economics (IUI).

Moon, H.C. (1994). A Revised Framework of Global Strategy: Extending the Coordination-Configuration Framework, *The International Executive*, 36(5): 557–573.

Moon, H.C. (1997). The Choice of Entry Modes and Theories of Foreign Direct Investment, *Journal of Global Marketing*, 11(2): 43–64.

Moon, H.C. (2004a). Cooperation among Japan, Korea and China Through Sharing Business and Cultural Advantages, *The Review of Business History*, 19(3): 33–51.

Moon, H.C. (2004b). The Evolution of Theories of Foreign Direct Investment, *The Review of Business History*, 19(1): 105–126.

Moon, H.C. (2004c). A Formal Modeling of the Imbalance Theory to Explain Two Directions of Foreign Direct Investment, *Journal of International Business and Economy*, 5(1): 117–132.

Moon, H.C. (2007). Outward Foreign Direct Investment by Enterprises from the Republic of Korea. In *Global Players from Emerging Markets: Strengthen Enterprise Competitiveness through Outward Investment,* New York and Geneva: United Nations.

Moon, H.C. (2010). *Global Business Strategy: Asian Perspective,* Singapore: World Scientific Publishing Co. Pte. Ltd.

Moon, H.C. (2012a). *Good to Smart,* Seoul: Rainmaker (in Korean).

Moon, H.C. (2012b). *The K-Strategy,* Seoul: Miraebook (in Korean).

Moon, H.C. (2014). The ABCD Framework of K-Strategy: The Secret to Korea's Success. Presented at *The Walter T. Shorenstein Asia-Pacific Research Center of Stanford University,* May 7, 2014. Available at http://aparc.stanford.edu/events/the_abcd_framework_of_kstrategy_the_secret_to_koreas_success/.

Moon, H.C. (2015, forthcoming). *The Strategy for Korea's Economic Success,* New York: Oxford University Press.

Moon, H.C., Rugman, A.M. and Verbeke, A. (1995). The Generalized Double Diamond Model Approach to International Competitiveness. In Rugman, A., Van Den Broeck, J. and Verbeke, A. (eds.), *Research in Global Strategic Management*: Beyond the Diamond (Volume 5), Greenwich, CT: JAI Press.

Moon, H.C., Rugman, A.M. and Verbeke, A. (1998). A Generalized Double Diamond Approach to the International Competitiveness of Korea and Singapore, *International Business Review,* 7(2): 135–150.

Moon, H.C. and Roehl, T.W. (2001). Unconventional Foreign Direct Investment and the Imbalance Theory, *International Business Review,* 10: 197–215.

Moon, H.C. and Jung, J.S. (2008). A Stage Approach to the Cluster Evolution and the Development of a New Global-Linking Cluster, *The Review of Business History,* 23(1): 77–104 (in Korean).

Moon, H.C. and Jung, J.S. (2010). Northeast Asian Cluster Through Business and Cultural Cooperation, *Journal of Korea Trade,* 14(2): 29–53.

Moon, H.C. and Kwon, D.B. (2010). Entry Mode Choice between Wholly-Owned Subsidiary and Joint Venture: A Case Study of the Automotive Industry in India, *International Journal of Performability Engineering,* 6(6): 605–614.

Moon, H.C. and Parc, J. (2014). The Economic Effects of Outward Foreign Direct Investment: A Case Study on Samsung Electronics Co., *Korean Business Review,* 18(3):125–145 (in Korean).

Moon, H.C., Parc, J., Yim, S. and Park, N. (2011). An Extension of Porter and Kramer's Creating Shared Value (CSV): Reorienting Strategies and Seeking International Cooperation, *Journal of International and Area Studies,* 18(2): 49–64.

Moon, H.C., Parc, J., Yim, S.H. and Yin, W. (2013). Enhancing Performability through Domestic and International Clustering: A Case Study of Samsung Electronics Corporation (SEC), *International Journal of Performability Engineering*, 9(1): 75–84.

Moon, H.C. and Yim, S.H. (2014). Reinterpreting the Ownership Advantages and Re-categorizing the Investment Motivations of Multinational Corporations: From the Perspective of Imbalance Theory, *Journal of International and Area Studies*, 21(1): 87–99.

Motoyama, Y. (2008). What Was New about the Cluster Theory? What Could it Answer and What Could it not Answer? *Economic Development Quarterly*, 22(4): 353–363.

Murray, E.A., Jr. (1976). The Social Response Process in Commercial Banks: An Empirical Investigation, *Academy of Management Review*, 1(3): 5–15.

Nachum, L. (2000). Economic Geography and the Location of TNCs: Financial and Professional Service FDI to the USA, *Journal of International Business Studies*, 31(3): 367–385.

Narula, R. (2010). Keeping the Eclectic Paradigm Simple, *Multinational Business Review*, 18(2):35–49.

Narula, R. and Dunning, J.H. (2000). Industrial Development, Globalization and Multinational Enterprises: New Realities for Developing Countries, *Oxford Development Studies*, 28(2): 141–167.

Negandhi, A.R. (1980). Multinational Corporations and Host Governments' Relationships: Comparative Study of Conflict and Conflicting Issues, *Human Relations*, 33(8): 517–541.

Nelson, R. and Winter, S. (1982). *An Evolutionary Theory of Economic Change*, Cambridge: Harvard University Press.

Netherlands Enterprise Agency (2011). *Suzhou Nanotechnology Overview*. Available at http://www.rvo.nl/sites/default/files/2013/09/Suzhou-Nanotechnology-Today.pdf.

Nisen, M. (2013). How Nike Solved Its Sweatshop Problem, *Business Insider*, May 9, 2013.

North, D.C. (1990). *Institutions, Institutional Change, and Economic Performance*, Cambridge: Harvard University Press.

Ohmae, K. (1985). *Triad Power: The Coming Shape of Global Competition*, New York: The Free Press.

Ohno, I. and Ohno, K. (2002). *Global Development Strategy and Japan's ODA Policy*, GRIPS Development Discussion Paper for the National Graduate Institute for Policy Studies.

Organization for Economic Co-Operation and Development (OECD) (2009). *Better Aid, Managing Aid: Practices of DAC Member Countries,* Paris: OECD.

Park, S.C. (2009). FDI in Services and the Productivity of Manufacturing: The Case of Korea, *International Commerce Research,* 14(2): 93–110.

Peng, M.W., Wang, D.Y.L. and Jiang, Y. (2008). An Institutions-Based View of International Business Strategy: A Focus on Emerging Economies, *Journal of International Business Studies,* 39: 920–936.

Penrose, E.T. (1956). Foreign Investment and the Growth of the Firm, *Economic Journal,* 66(June): 220–235.

Penrose, E.T. (1959). *The Theory of the Growth of the Firm,* Oxford: Basil Blackwell.

Perlmutter, H.V. (1969). The Tortuous Evolution of the Multinational Corporation, *Columbia Journal of World Business,* 4(4): 9–18.

Pisano, G.P. (1994). Knowledge, Integration, and the Locus of Learning: An Empirical Analysis of Process Development, *Strategic Management Journal,* 15(Winter Special Issue): 85–100.

Pitelis, C.N. and Teece, D.J. (2010). Cross-Border Market Co-Creation, Dynamic Capabilities and the Entrepreneurial Theory of the Multinational Enterprise, *Industrial Corporate Change,* 19(4): 1247–1270.

Porter, M.E. (1980). Industry Structure and Competitive Strategy: Keys to Profitability, *Financial Analysts Journal,* 36(4): 30–41.

Porter, M.E. (1985). *Competitive Advantage: Creating and Sustaining Superior Performance,* New York: Free Press.

Porter, M.E. (1986). *Competition in Global Industries,* Boston: Harvard Business School Press.

Porter, M.E. (1990). *The Competitive Advantage of Nations,* New York: Free Press.

Porter, M.E. (1994). The Role of Location in Competition, *Journal of the Economics of Business,* 1(1): 35–39.

Porter, M.E. (1996). What Is Strategy? *Harvard Business Review,* 74(6): 61–78.

Porter, M.E. (1998a). Clusters and the New Economics of Competition, *Harvard Business Review,* 76(6): 77–90.

Porter, M.E. (1998b). Clusters and the New Competitive Agenda for Companies and Government. In Porter, M.E. (ed.), *On Competition,* Boston: Harvard Business School Press.

Porter, M.E. (2000a). Attitudes, Values, Beliefs, and the Microeconomics of Prosperity. In Harrison, L.E. and Huntington, S.P. (eds.), *Culture Matters: How Values Shape Human Progress,* New York: Basic Books.

Porter, M.E. (2000b). Location, Competition, and Economic Development: Local Clusters in a Global Economy, *Economic Development Quarterly,* 14(1): 15–34.

Porter, M.E. and Kramer, M.R. (2002). The Competitive Advantage of Corporate Philanthropy, *Harvard Business Review*, 80: 56–69.

Porter, M.E. and Kramer, M.R. (2006). Strategy and Society: The Link between Competitive Advantage and Corporate Social Responsibility, *Harvard Business Review*, 84: 78–92.

Porter, M.E. and Kramer, M.R. (2011). Creating Shared Value, *Harvard Business Review*, 89(1/2): 62–77.

Portes, A. and Sensenbrenner, J. (1993). Embeddedness and Immigration: Notes on the Social Determinants of Economic Action, *American Journal of Sociology*, 98(6): 1320–1350.

Potterie, B.V.P. and Lichtenberg, F. (2001). Does Foreign Direct Investment Transfer Technology across Borders?, *Review of Economics and Statistics*, 83(3): 490–497.

Prahalad, C.K. and Doz, Y.L. (1987). *The Multinational Mission: Balancing Global Integration with Local Responsiveness*, New York: The Free Press.

Prickett, G. (2003). *Can Corporations–NGO Partnerships Save the Environment* (Part 1). Available at http://www.onlineopinion.com.au/view.sp?article=1180.

Political Risk Service Group (PRSG) (2014a). *PRS methodology*. Available at http://www.prsgroup.com/PRS_Methodology.aspx.

Political Risk Service Group (PRSG) (2014b). *ICRG Methodology*. Available at http://www.prsgroup.com/ICRG_Methodology.aspx.

Raisch, S., Birkinshaw, J., Probst, G. and Tushman, M.L. (2009). Organizational Ambidexterity: Balancing Exploitation and Exploration for Sustained Performance, *Organization Science*, 20(4): 685–695.

Rasheed, H.S. (2005). Foreign Entry Mode and Performance: The Moderating Effects of Environment, *Journal of Small Business Management*, 43(1): 41–54.

Rayport, J.F. and Sviokla, J.J. (1995). Exploiting the Virtual Value Chain, *Harvard Business Review*, 73(6): 75–85.

Redding, G. (2005). The Thick Description and Comparison of Societal Systems of Capitalism, *Journal of International Business Studies*, 36(2): 123–155.

Reich R.B. (1990). Who is Us?, *Harvard Business Review*, 68(1): 53–64.

Reich, R.B. (1991). Who is Them?, *Harvard Business Review*, 69(2): 77–88.

Richardson, E.L. (2011). United States Policy toward Foreign Direct Investment: We Can't Have It Both Ways, *American University International Law Review*, 4(2): 281–317.

Ring, P.S. and Van de Ven, A.H. (1994). Developing Processes of Cooperative Inter-Organizational Relationships, *Academy of Management Review*, 19(1): 90–118.

Romo, F.P. and Schwartz, M. (1995). Structural Embeddedness of Business Decisions: A Sociological Assessment of the Migration Behavior of Plants in

New York State between 1960 and 1985, *American Sociological Review,* 60: 864–907.

Ronen, S. and Shenkar, O. (1985). Clustering Countries on Attitudinal Dimension: A Review and Synthesis, *Academy of Management Review,* 10(3): 435–454.

Root, F.R. (1987). *Entry Strategies for International Market,* Lexington: Heath.

Rugman, A.M. (1979). *International Diversification and the Multinational Enterprise,* Lexington: Lexington Books.

Rugman, A.M. (1980). Internalization as a General Theory of Foreign Direct Investment: A Re-Appraisal of the Literature, *Review of World Economics,* 116(2): 365–379.

Rugman, A.M. (1981). *Inside the Multinationals: The Economics of Internal Markets,* Columbia: Columbia University Press.

Rugman, A. M. and Verbeke, A. (2002). Edith Penrose's Contribution to the Resource-Based View of Strategic Management, *Strategic Management Journal,* 23(8): 769–780.

Rugman, A.M. and Verbeke, A. (2004). A Perspective on Regional and Global Strategies of Multinational Enterprises, *Journal of International Business Studies,* 35: 3–18.

Rugman, A.M. and Verbeke, A. (2008). A New Perspective on the Regional and Global Strategies of Multinational Services Firms, *Management International Review,* 48(4): 397–411.

Salomon, R.M. and Shaver, J.M. (2005). Learning by Exporting: New Insights from Examining firm Innovation, *Journal of Economics & Management Strategy,* 14(2): 431–460.

Samsung (2003). *Samsung Electronics Adds New Production Line and R&D Center to Suzhou, China Facility.* Available at http://www.samsung.com/global/business/semiconductor/news-events/press-releases/detail?newsId=4319.

Samsung (2011). *Samsung Expanding Presence in LCD Market in China.* Available at http://www.samsung.com/us/news/19860.

Saxenian, A. (1994). *Regional Advantage: Culture and Competition in Silicon Valley and Rout 128,* Cambridge: Harvard University Press.

Scheve, K.F. and Slaughter, M.J. (2004). Economic Insecurity and the Globalization of Production, *American Journal of Political Science,* 48(4): 662–674.

Schmitz, H. (1995). Small Shoemakers and Fordist Giants: Tale of a Supercluster, *World Development,* 23(1): 9–28.

Schmid, S. and Grosche, P. (2013). *Managing the International Value Chain in the Automotive Industry,* Gütersloh: Bertelsmann Stiftung.

Schumpeter, J.A. (1934). *The Theory of Economic Development,* Cambridge: Harvard University Press.

Scott, A.J. (1998). *Regions and the World Economy: The Coming Shape of World Production, Competition, and Political Order,* Oxford and New York: Oxford University Press.

Seoul National University (2009). *Examining the Investment Attractiveness,* Presented at the Ministry of Knowledge Economy (in Korean).

Sethi, S.P. (1975). Dimensions of Corporate Social Performance: An Analytic Framework, *California Management Review,* 17: 58–64.

Sethi, D. Guisinger, S.E., Phelan, S.E. and Berg, D.M. (2003). Trends in Foreign Direct Investment Flows: A Theoretical and Empirical Analysis, *Journal of International Business Studies,* 34: 315–326.

Shenkar, O. (2001). Cultural Distance Revisited: Towards a More Rigorous Conceptualization and Measurement of Cultural Differences, *Journal of International Business Studies,* 32(3): 519–535.

Smit, A.J. (2010). The Competitive Advantage of Nations: Is Porter's Diamond Framework a New Theory that Explains the International Competitiveness of Countries?, *Southern African Business Review,* 14(1): 105–130.

Soule-Kohndou, F. (2013). *The India–Brazil–South Africa Forum a Decade on: Mismatched Partners or the Rise of the South?* The Global Economic Governance Programme Working Paper 2013/88, November 2013.

Storper, M. (1997). *The Regional World: Territorial Development in a Global Economy,* New York: Guilford Press.

Sumantoro (1984). *MNCs and the Host Country: The Indonesian Case,* Research Notes and Discussion Papers, No.45, Singapore: Institute of Southeast Asian Studies.

Sunaga, K. (2004). *The Reshaping of Japan's Official Development Assistance (ODA) Charter,* Discussion Paper on Development Assistance, No.3, November 2004.

Suwonilbo. (2010). *Samsung Settled Down in Suwon.* Available at http://www.suwon.com/news/articleView.html?idxno=46335 (in Korean).

Taylor, F.W. (1967). *The Principles of Scientific Management,* New York: Norton.

Teece, D.J. (1986a). Transaction Cost Economics and the Multinational Enterprise: An Assessment, *Journal of Economic Behavior and Organization,* 7: 21–45.

Teece, D.J. (1986b). Profiting from Technological Innovation: Implications for Integration, Collaboration, Licensing and Public Policy, *Research Policy,* 15: 285–305.

Teece, D.J. (1992). Competition, Cooperation, and Innovation; Organizational Arrangements for Regimes of Rapid Technological Progress, *Journal of Economic Behavior and Organization,* 18: 1–25.

Teece, D.J. (2007). Explicating Dynamic Capabilities: The Nature and Microfoundations of (Sustainable) Enterprise Performance, *Strategic Management Journal,* 28(13): 1319–1350.

Teece, D.J., Pisano, G. and Shuen, A. (1997). Dynamic Capabilities and Strategic Management, *Strategic Management Journal*, 18(7): 509–533.

Tekes (2010). *Suzhou Innovation Ecosystem*. Available at http://www.tekes.fi/en/programmes-and-services/campaigns/nanochina/suzhou/.

The Institute for Industrial Policy Studies (IPS) (2012). *Promoting Foreign Direct Investment (FDI) in Azerbaijan*, Project for the Ministry of Economic Development (MED), Republic of Azerbaijan.

The Wall Street Journal and The Heritage Foundation (2013). *Methodology*. Available at http://www.heritage.org/index/book/methodology.

Tsai, W. and Ghoshal, S. (1998). Social Capital and Value Creation: The Role of Inter-Firm Networks, *Academy of Management Journal*, 41(4): 464–476.

Tushman, M.L. and O'Reilly, C.A. (1996). The Ambidextrous Organization: Managing Evolutionary and Revolutionary Change, *California Management Review*, 38: 1–23.

UNCTAD (1995). *World Invest Reports, Transnational Corporations and Competitiveness*, New York and Geneva: UNCTAD.

UNCTAD (1999). *World Invest Reports, Foreign Direct Investment and the Challenge of Development*, New York and Geneva: UNCTAD.

UNCTAD (2000). *World Invest Reports, Cross-Border Mergers and Acquisitions and Development*, New York and Geneva: UNCTAD.

UNCTAD (2002). *World Invest Reports, Transnational Corporations and Export Competitiveness*, New York and Geneva: UNCTAD.

UNCTAD (2006). *World Invest Reports, FDI from Developing and Transition Economies: Implications for Development*, New York and Geneva: UNCTAD.

UNCTAD (2012). *World Invest Reports, Towards a New Generation of Investment Policies*, New York and Geneva: UNCTAD.

UNCTAD (2013). *World Invest Reports, Global Value Chains: Investment and Trade for Development*, New York and Geneva: UNCTAD.

USDA (2012). *U.S. Textile and Apparel Industries and Rural America*. Available at http://www.ers.usda.gov/topics/crops/cotton-wool/background/us-textile-and-apparel-industries-and-rural-america.aspx#.U4hAZPl_vhA.

Uzzi, B. (1997). Social Structure and Competition in Interfirm Networks: The Paradox of Embeddedness, *Administrative Science Quarterly*, 42(1): 35–67.

Verdict. (2012). *The Verdict Website*. Available at http://www.verdictretail.com/nissans-sunderland-plant-expansion-offers-opportunities-for-uk-supply-chain/.

Vogel, D.J. (2005). Is there a Market for Virtue? The Business Case for Corporate Social Responsibility, *California Management Review*, 47(4): 19–45.

Weber, A. (1929). *Theory of the Location of Industries*, Chicago: The University of Chicago Press.

Wernerfelt, B. (1984). A Resource-based View of the Firm, *Strategic Management Journal*, 5: 171–180.

Williamson, O.E. (1975). *Markets and Hierarchies: Analysis and Antitrust Implications*, New York: Free Press.

Williamson, O.E. (1981). The Modern Corporation: Origins, Evolution, Attributes, *Journal of Economic Literature*, 19(4): 1537–1568.

Williamson, O.E. (1985). *The Economic Institutions of Capitalism*, New York: The Free Press.

Williamson, O.E. (1991). Comparative Economic Organization: The Analysis of Discrete Structural Alternatives, *Administrative Science Quarterly*, 36(2): 269–296.

Winter, S.G. (2003). Understanding Dynamic Capabilities, *Strategic Management Journal*, 24: 991–995.

World Bank (1993). *The East Asian Miracle: Economic Growth and Public Policy*, Washington, D.C.: World Bank.

World Bank. (2005). *Global Development Finance: Mobilizing Finance and Managing Vulnerability*, Washington, DC: World Bank.

World Bank. (2013). *Ease of Doing Business and Distance to Frontier*. Available at http://www.doingbusiness.org/methodology.

World Economic Forum (WEF) (2013). *The Global Competitiveness Report* 2013–2014, Geneva: WEF.

Xu, D., Pan, Y., Wu, C. and Yim, B. (2006). Performance of Domestic and Foreign-Invested Enterprises in China, *Journal of World Business*, 41(3): 261–274.

Yang, H. (2006). Benchmarking Alabama Governments' Commitment to Foreign Companies in the Auto Industry. College of Northeast Asian Studies, University of Incheon (Working paper). April 7.

Yazji, M. (2006). *Sleeping with the Enemy for Competitive Advantage: Corporation and NGO Partnerships*, Geneva: IMD International.

Yehoue, E.B. (2005). *Clusters as a Driving Engine for FDI*, Washington, D.C.: International Monetary Fund (IMF).

Yim, S.H. (2013). Moving beyond FDI and Clusters: Platform Perspective Toward Mutual Value Creation, *Journal of International Business and Economy*, 14(2): 49–67.

Yiu, D.W., Lau, C.M. and Bruton, G.D. (2007). International Venturing by Emerging Economy Firms: The Effects of Firm Capabilities, Home Country Networks, and Corporate Entrepreneurship, *Journal of International Business Studies*, 38: 519–540.

Young, S., Huang, C. and McDermott, M. (1996). Internationalization and Competitive Catchup Processes: Case Study Evidence on Chinese Multinational Enterprises, *Management International Review*, 36(4): 295–314.

Zahra, S.A. and George, G. (2002). Absorptive Capacity: A Review, Reconceptualization, and Extension, *Academy of Management Review,* 27(2): 185–203.

Zollo, M. and Winter, S.G. (2002). Deliberate Learning and the Evolution of Dynamic Capabilities, *Organization Science,* 13: 339–351.

Epilogue

The most popular theory of FDI has been Dunning's eclectic theory or OLI paradigm, which has been a very useful tool for explaining the downward FDI from more developed country to less developed country in a rather simple world focusing on just the relationship between the MNC and host country's market failure. In today's more complicated world where FDI motivations are more diverse than ever, each of the OLI variables needs to be extended to better explain the changing patterns of MNC operations.

First, the "O" advantage, which focuses on the exploitation of MNC resources, has to incorporate new FDI motivations of "sharing and learning" between firms and countries. The MNC is not an exploiter but an agent to "balance out" any imbalances between firms and countries (Moon and Roehl, 2001).

Second, the "L" advantage, which treats only factor conditions (i.e., resource-seeking, efficiency-seeking, and asset-seeking) and demand conditions (i.e., market-seeking), should also incorporate other motivations, such as supporting sectors and business context of the (double) diamond model determinants (Moon, 2007).

Third, the "I" advantage, which deals only with "internalization", needs to incorporate "externalization" as well because firms choose different strategies in a similar condition of market failure (e.g., Samsung Electronics prefers internalization, while Apple chooses externalization in the same smart phone industry).

The most important change in the competitive pattern of international business is the scope of competition: from individual MNC to MNC's global value chain. In the global competition, for example, Samsung Electronics does not compete against its suppliers or other component providers. Rather Samsung Electronics, together with all of its partnering firms, competes against Apple's value chain on a global scale. In reality, Samsung Electronics has made huge investments in Vietnam, which are more complementary with than substituting for Samsung's operation in Korea on a global basis. The future task of global managers is not how to exploit the host country but how to build an efficient global value chain which can synergistically integrate the competitive advantages of the firm, home and host countries.

Index

Printed in the United States
By Bookmasters